CliffsQuickReview™
Principles of
Management

By Ellen A. Benowitz, M Ed

WILEY

Wiley Publishing, Inc.

About the Author

Professor Ellen A. Benowitz has been employed at Mercer County Community College since 1972. In addition to providing instruction in the areas of accounting, business organization, business communications and management, she has also served in several administrative positions. Professor Benowitz is also the New Jersey State Chairman for Future Business Leaders of America-Phi Beta Lambda and serves as member of the national board of directors.

Publisher's Acknowledgments

Editorial

Project Editors: Kathleen A. Dobie, Allyson Grove

Acquisitions Editor: Gregory W. Tubach

Copy Editor: Ellen Considine

Technical Editor: Dr. Patricia Barchi

Editorial Assistants: Melissa Bennett, Jennifer Young

Composition

Indexer: TECHBOOKS Production Services

Proofreader: TECHBOOKS Production Services

Wiley Indianapolis Composition Services

CliffsQuickReview™ Principles of Management

Published by
Wiley Publishing, Inc.
111 River Street
Hoboken, NJ 07030
www.wiley.com

Table of Contents

INTRODUCTION

You are about to begin studying one of the most important and interesting disciplines of business — the field of management. What an exciting time to be a student of management! Times are changing, and so are the functions and roles of the manager. Tomorrow's managers must be prepared to meet the challenges of a highly dynamic and rapidly changing business environment.

Whether you're a new managerial professional or a student who has decided upon a career in business, government, or educational management, this book provides a valuable introduction to the concepts of management and business. It provides essential skills in planning and organizing, staffing and directing, controlling, decision making, motivating, communicating, and applying managerial skills to business and other types of organization.

Why You Need This Book

Can you answer yes to any of these questions?

- Do you need to review the fundamentals of management fast?

- Do you need a course supplement to Introduction to Management?

- Do you need a concise, comprehensive reference for Introduction to Management?

If so, then CliffsQuickReview *Principles of Management* is for you!

How to Use This Book

You can use this book in any way that fits your personal style for study and review — you decide what works best with your needs. You can either read the book from cover to cover or just look for the information you want and put it back on the shelf for later. Here are just a few ways you can search for topics:

- Use the Pocket Guide to find essential information, such as the terminology used by managers, concepts important to managers, and laws that managers must adhere to.

- Look for areas of interest in the book's Table of Contents, or use the index to find specific topics.

- Flip through the book looking for subject areas at the top of each page.

- Get a glimpse of what you'll gain from a chapter by reading through the "Chapter Check-In" at the beginning of each chapter.

- Use the Chapter Checkout at the end of each chapter to gauge your grasp of the important information you need to know.

- Test your knowledge more completely in the CQR Review and look for additional sources of information in the CQR Resource Center.

- Use the glossary to find key terms fast. This book defines new terms and concepts where they first appear in the chapter. If a word is bold-faced, you can find a more complete definition in the book's glossary.

- Or flip through the book until you find what you're looking for — we organized this book to gradually build on key concepts.

Visit Our Web Site

A great resource, `www.cliffsnotes.com`, features review materials, valuable Internet links, quizzes, and more to enhance your learning. The site also features timely articles and tips, plus downloadable versions of many CliffsNotes books.

When you stop by our site, don't hesitate to share your thoughts about this book or any Wiley product. Just click the Talk to Us button. We welcome your feedback!

Chapter 1

THE NATURE OF MANAGEMENT

Chapter Check-In

❑ Defining management

❑ Identifying management levels and functions

❑ Evaluating managers' many roles

❑ Describing different management skills

❑ Avoiding management myths

In today's tough and uncertain economy, a company needs strong managers to lead its staff toward accomplishing business goals. But managers are more than just leaders — they're problem solvers, cheerleaders, and planners as well. And managers don't come in one-size-fits-all shapes or forms. Managers fulfill many roles and have many different responsibilities at each level of management within an organization. In this chapter, you not only discover those roles and functions, but you also find out the truth about several common misconceptions about management.

Management and Organizations

Organizations abound in today's society. Groups of individuals constantly join forces to accomplish common goals. Sometimes the goals of these organizations are for profit, such as franchise restaurant chains or clothing retailers. Other times, the goals are more altruistic, such as nonprofit churches or public schools. But no matter what their aims, all these organizations share two things in common: They're made up of people, and certain individuals are in charge of these people.

Enter managers. **Managers** appear in every organization — at least in organizations that want to succeed. These individuals have the sometimes-unenviable task of making decisions, solving difficult problems, setting goals, planning strategies, and rallying individuals. And those are just a few of their responsibilities!

To be exact, managers administer and coordinate resources effectively and efficiently to achieve the goals of an organization. In essence, managers get the job done through other people.

The intricacies of management

No matter what type of organization they work in, managers are generally responsible for a group of individuals' performance. As leaders, managers must encourage this group to reach common business goals, such as bringing a new product to market in a timely fashion. To accomplish these goals, managers not only use their human resources, but they also take advantage of various material resources as well, such as technology.

Think of a team, for example. A manager may be in charge of a certain department whose task it is to develop a new product. The manager needs to coordinate the efforts of his department's team members, as well as give them the material tools they need to accomplish the job well. If the team fails, ultimately it is the manager who shoulders the responsibility.

Levels of management

Two leaders may serve as managers within the same company but have very different titles and purposes. Large organizations, in particular, may break down management into different levels because so many more people need to be managed. Typical management levels fall into the following categories:

- Top level: Managers at this level ensure that major performance objectives are established and accomplished. Common job titles for top managers include chief executive officer (CEO), chief operating officer (COO), president, and vice president. These senior managers are considered executives, responsible for the performance of an organization as a whole or for one of its significant parts. When you think of a top-level manager, think of someone like Dave Thomas of the fast-food franchise Wendy's. Although John T. Schuessler was elected CEO in 2000, Dave Thomas is the founder and still the chairman of the board. He is the well-known spokesperson for the chain.

- **Middle level:** Middle managers report to top managers and are in charge of relatively large departments or divisions consisting of several smaller units. Examples of middle managers include clinic directors in hospitals; deans in universities; and division managers, plant managers, and branch sales managers in businesses. Middle managers develop and implement action plans consistent with company objectives, such as increasing market presence.

■ **Low level:** The initial management job that most people attain is typically a **first-line management** position, such as a team leader or supervisor — a person in charge of smaller work units composed of hands-on workers. Job titles for these first-line managers vary greatly, but include such designations as department head, group leader, and unit leader. First-line managers ensure that their work teams or units meet performance objectives, such as producing a set number of items at a given quality, that are consistent with the plans of middle and top management.

Functions of Managers

Managers just don't go out and haphazardly perform their responsibilities. Good managers discover how to master five basic functions: planning, organizing, staffing, leading, and controlling.

■ **Planning:** This step involves mapping out exactly how to achieve a particular goal. Say, for example, that the organization's goal is to improve company sales. The manager first needs to decide which steps are necessary to accomplish that goal. These steps may include increasing advertising, inventory, and sales staff. These necessary steps are developed into a plan. When the plan is in place, the manager can follow it to accomplish the goal of improving company sales.

■ **Organizing:** After a plan is in place, a manager needs to organize her team and materials according to her plan. Assigning work and granting authority are two important elements of organizing.

■ **Staffing:** After a manager discerns his area's needs, he may decide to beef up his staffing by recruiting, selecting, training, and developing employees. A manager in a large organization often works with the company's human resources department to accomplish this goal.

■ **Leading:** A manager needs to do more than just plan, organize, and staff her team to achieve a goal. She must also lead. Leading involves motivating, communicating, guiding, and encouraging. It requires the manager to coach, assist, and problem solve with employees.

■ **Controlling:** After the other elements are in place, a manager's job is not finished. He needs to continuously check results against goals and take any corrective actions necessary to make sure that his area's plans remain on track.

All managers at all levels of every organization perform these functions, but the amount of time a manager spends on each one depends on both the level of management and the specific organization.

Roles performed by managers

A manager wears many hats. Not only is a manager a team leader, but he or he is also a planner, organizer, cheerleader, coach, problem solver, and decision maker — all rolled into one. And these are just a few of a manger's roles.

In addition, managers' schedules are usually jam-packed. Whether they're busy with employee meetings, unexpected problems, or strategy sessions, managers often find little spare time on their calendars. (And that doesn't even include responding to e-mail!)

In his classic book, *The Nature of Managerial Work,* Henry Mintzberg describes a set of ten roles that a manager fills. These roles fall into three categories:

■ **Interpersonal:** This role involves human interaction.

■ **Informational:** This role involves the sharing and analyzing of information.

■ **Decisional:** This role involves decision making.

Table 1-1 contains a more in-depth look at each category of roles that help managers carry out all five functions described in the preceding "Functions of managers" section.

Table 1-1   Mintzberg's Set of Ten Roles

Category	Role	Activity
Informational	Monitor	Seek and receive information; scan periodicals and reports; maintain personal contact with stakeholders.
	Disseminator	Forward information to organization members via memos, reports, and phone calls.
	Spokesperson	Transmit information to outsiders via reports, memos, and speeches.

Category	Role	Activity
Interpersonal	Figurehead	Perform ceremonial and symbolic duties, such as greeting visitors and signing legal documents.
	Leader	Direct and motivate subordinates; counsel and communicate with subordinates.
	Liaison	Maintain information links both inside and outside organization via mail, phone calls, and meetings.
Decisional	Entrepreneur	Initiate improvement projects; identify new ideas and delegate idea responsibility to others.
	Disturbance handler	Take corrective action during disputes or crises; resolve conflicts among subordinates; adapt to environments.
	Resource allocator	Decide who gets resources; prepare budgets; set schedules and determine priorities.
	Negotiator	Represent department during negotiations of union contracts, sales, purchases, and budgets.

Skills needed by managers

Not everyone can be a manager. Certain **skills,** or abilities to translate knowledge into action that results in desired performance, are required to help other employees become more productive. These skills fall under the following categories:

- ■ **Technical:** This skill requires the ability to use a special proficiency or expertise to perform particular tasks. Accountants, engineers, market researchers, and computer scientists, as examples, possess technical skills. Managers acquire these skills initially through formal education and then further develop them through training and job experience. Technical skills are most important at lower levels of management.

- ■ **Human:** This skill demonstrates the ability to work well in cooperation with others. Human skills emerge in the workplace as a spirit of trust, enthusiasm, and genuine involvement in interpersonal relationships. A manager with good human skills has a high degree of self-awareness and a capacity to understand or empathize with the feelings of others. Some managers are naturally born with great human skills, while others improve their skills through classes or experience. No matter how human skills are acquired, they're critical for all managers because of the highly interpersonal nature of managerial work.

■ **Conceptual:** This skill calls for the ability to think analytically. Analytical skills enable managers to break down problems into smaller parts, to see the relations among the parts, and to recognize the implications of any one problem for others. As managers assume ever-higher responsibilities in organizations, they must deal with more ambiguous problems that have long-term consequences. Again, managers may acquire these skills initially through formal education and then further develop them by training and job experience. The higher the management level, the more important conceptual skills become.

Although all three categories contain skills essential for managers, their relative importance tends to vary by level of managerial responsibility.

Business and management educators are increasingly interested in helping people acquire technical, human, and conceptual skills, and develop specific competencies, or specialized skills, that contribute to high performance in a management job. Following are some of the skills and personal characteristics that the American Assembly of Collegiate Schools of Business (AACSB) is urging business schools to help their students develop.

■ **Leadership** — ability to influence others to perform tasks

■ **Self-objectivity** — ability to evaluate yourself realistically

■ **Analytic thinking** — ability to interpret and explain patterns in information

■ **Behavioral flexibility** — ability to modify personal behavior to react objectively rather than subjectively to accomplish organizational goals.

■ **Oral communication** — ability to express ideas clearly in words

■ **Written communication** — ability to express ideas clearly in writing

■ **Personal impact** — ability to create a good impression and instill confidence

■ **Resistance to stress** — ability to perform under stressful conditions

■ **Tolerance for uncertainty** — ability to perform in ambiguous situations

Dispelling Common Management Myths

Some employees have a hard time describing exactly what their managers do on a typical day. Because managers aren't always seen doing tangible hands-on work, such as writing a computer program, editing a book, or selling a product, sometimes employees think they do nothing but sit and wait for problems to arise. But that misconception is just one of several myths that are very different from the many realities of management. The following examples discuss not only the most common myths about managers but also the realities.

■ **Myth:** *The manager is a reflective, methodical planner.*

■ **Reality:** The average manager is swamped by trivialities and crises and spends only nine minutes or so on any activity.

■ **Myth:** *The effective manager has no regular duties to perform.*

■ **Reality:** Managers attend upper management meetings, meet regularly with employees, coworkers, and potential clients, and absorb and process information on a continued basis.

■ **Myth:** *The manager's job is a science.*

■ **Reality:** Managers rely heavily on interaction and judgment.

■ **Myth:** *Managers are self-starters, self-directed, and autonomous.*

■ **Reality:** Good managers are self-managing: They accept autonomy, while seeking input from supervisors.

■ **Myth:** *Good managers seek out the information they require.*

■ **Reality:** Managers don't always have access to information they need.

■ **Myth:** *Competition among managers is good for business.*

■ **Reality:** Collaboration (the pooling of resources) and cooperation (working together) among managers creates a better business. Today, the concepts of TQM (which are discussed in Chapter 15) indicate that organizations function better if resources and knowledge are shared and individuals work together as a team.

Uncovering your own beliefs of management is important as you develop an awareness of "true" daily management duties.

Chapter Checkout

Q&A

1. For most organizations, top management consists of _____.
   a. any manager above the level of foreman
   b. the chief executive officer, the president, and his or her vice presidents
   c. the chief executive officer only
   d. the chief executive officer and the president only

2. The management functions are _____.
   a. planning, organizing, staffing, leading, and controlling
   b. organizing, selling, accounting, leading, and controlling
   c. planning, accounting, controlling, leading, and organizing
   d. planning, organizing, selling, leading, and controlling

3. The categories of management roles are _____.
   a. figurehead, leader, and liaison
   b. monitor, disseminator, and spokesperson
   c. interpersonal, decisional, and entrepreneur
   d. interpersonal, informational, and decisional

4. The skills that all managers need are _____.
   a. planning, organizing, and controlling
   b. conceptual, technical, and human
   c. effectiveness, efficiency, and planning
   d. interpersonal, decisional, and informational

5. Which of the following is a reality of a manager's job?
   a. A manager's job is less a science than an art.
   b. Managers are self-starting, self-directing, and autonomous.
   c. Managers have no regular duties to perform.
   d. Managers are reflective and systematic planners.

Answers: 1. b **2.** a **3.** d **4.** b **5.** a

Chapter 2

THE EVOLUTION OF MANAGEMENT THOUGHT

Chapter Check-In

- ❑ Discovering the different schools of management
- ❑ Introducing human resource approaches
- ❑ Identifying the role of quantitative analysis
- ❑ Understanding contingency thinking
- ❑ Focusing on quality
- ❑ Looking forward to the future of management

Harley-Davidson, an 80-year-old motorcycle manufacturer, experienced a rather dramatic reversal of its fortunes during the late 1970s and early 1980s when its market share slipped to less than 4 percent. Honda, Kawasaki, and Yamaha motorcycles had come roaring into America from Japan, offering not only low prices but also higher quality, state-of-the-art machines.

At first, Harley-Davidson accused Japan of selling below cost just to get its motorcycles into the American market. But Harley-Davidson's president Vaughn Beals later found out that in reality, Japan was able to manufacture its cycles at a 30 percent lower cost than Harley-Davidson was. After some careful investigation, Beals found that Harley-Davidson was using outmoded production technology. In addition, the organization's structure was cumbersome, and employees were viewed as nothing but muscle needed to carry out the assigned duties.

In light of this, Harley-Davidson began to realize that the management style, organizational structure, and production technologies that had worked in the past weren't going to be successful in the future. In fact, if the management philosophy didn't change, the long-term survival of the company would be in doubt.

As the Harley-Davidson example illustrates, the ever-changing business environment has forced management thinking to evolve throughout the centuries. This chapter examines the evolution of management thought by describing several management theories and philosophies that have emerged over the years. Most of the evolutionary changes and new perspectives occurred as a result of the Industrial Revolution that transformed agricultural societies into industrial societies. Today, management thinking continues to evolve to meet the challenges of rapid and dramatic societal changes.

Classical Schools of Management

One of the first schools of management thought, the **classical management theory,** developed during the Industrial Revolution when new problems related to the factory system began to appear. Managers were unsure of how to train employees (many of them non-English speaking immigrants) or deal with increased labor dissatisfaction, so they began to test solutions. As a result, the classical management theory developed from efforts to find the "one best way" to perform and manage tasks. This school of thought is made up of two branches: classical scientific and classical administrative, described in the following sections.

Classical scientific school

The **classical scientific branch** arose because of the need to increase productivity and efficiency. The emphasis was on trying to find the best way to get the most work done by examining how the work process was actually accomplished and by scrutinizing the skills of the workforce.

The classical scientific school owes its roots to several major contributors, including Frederick Taylor, Henry Gantt, and Frank and Lillian Gilbreth.

Frederick Taylor is often called the "father of scientific management." Taylor believed that organizations should study tasks and develop precise procedures. As an example, in 1898, Taylor calculated how much iron from rail cars Bethlehem Steel plant workers could be unloading if they were using the correct movements, tools, and steps. The result was an amazing 47.5 tons per day instead of the mere 12.5 tons each worker had been averaging. In addition, by redesigning the shovels the workers used, Taylor was able to increase the length of work time and therefore decrease the number of people shoveling from 500 to 140. Lastly, he developed an incentive system that paid workers more money for meeting the new standard. Productivity at Bethlehem Steel shot up overnight. As a result, many theorists followed Taylor's philosophy when developing their own principles of management.

Henry Gantt, an associate of Taylor's, developed the Gantt chart, a bar graph that measures planned and completed work along each stage of production. Based on time instead of quantity, volume, or weight, this visual display chart has been a widely used planning and control tool since its development in 1910.

Frank and Lillian Gilbreth, a husband-and-wife team, studied job motions. In Frank's early career as an apprentice bricklayer, he was interested in standardization and method study. He watched bricklayers and saw that some workers were slow and inefficient, while others were very productive. He discovered that each bricklayer used a different set of motions to lay bricks. From his observations, Frank isolated the basic movements necessary to do the job and eliminated unnecessary motions. Workers using these movements raised their output from 1,000 to 2,700 bricks per day. This was the first **motion study** designed to isolate the best possible method of performing a given job. Later, Frank and his wife Lillian studied job motions using a motion-picture camera and a split-second clock. When her husband died at the age of 56, Lillian continued their work.

Thanks to these contributors and others, the basic ideas regarding scientific management developed. They include the following:

- Developing new standard methods for doing each job

- Selecting, training, and developing workers instead of allowing them to choose their own tasks and train themselves

- Developing a spirit of cooperation between workers and management to ensure that work is carried out in accordance with devised procedures

- Dividing work between workers and management in almost equal shares, with each group taking over the work for which it is best fitted

Classical administrative school

Whereas scientific management focused on the productivity of individuals, the classical administrative approach concentrates on the total organization. The emphasis is on the development of managerial principles rather than work methods.

Contributors to this school of thought include Max Weber, Henri Fayol, Mary Parker Follett, and Chester I. Barnard. These theorists studied the flow of information within an organization and emphasized the importance of understanding how an organization operated.

In the late 1800s, **Max Weber** disliked that many European organizations were managed on a "personal" family-like basis and that employees were loyal to individual supervisors rather than to the organization. He believed that organizations should be managed impersonally and that a formal organizational structure, where specific rules were followed, was important. In other words, he didn't think that authority should be based on a person's personality. He thought authority should be something that was part of a person's job and passed from individual to individual as one person left and another took over. This nonpersonal, objective form of organization was called a **bureaucracy.**

Weber believed that all bureaucracies have the following characteristics:

- **A well-defined hierarchy.** All positions within a bureaucracy are structured in a way that permits the higher positions to supervise and control the lower positions. This clear chain of command facilitates control and order throughout the organization.

- **Division of labor and specialization.** All responsibilities in an organization are specialized so that each employee has the necessary expertise to do a particular task.

- **Rules and regulations.** Standard operating procedures govern all organizational activities to provide certainty and facilitate coordination.

- **Impersonal relationships between managers and employees.** Managers should maintain an impersonal relationship with employees so that favoritism and personal prejudice do not influence decisions.

- **Competence.** Competence, not "who you know," should be the basis for all decisions made in hiring, job assignments, and promotions in order to foster ability and merit as the primary characteristics of a bureaucratic organization.

- **Records.** A bureaucracy needs to maintain complete files regarding all its activities.

Henri Fayol, a French mining engineer, developed 14 principles of management based on his management experiences. These principles provide modern-day managers with general guidelines on how a supervisor should organize her department and manage her staff. Although later research has created controversy over many of the following principles, they are still widely used in management theories.

- **Division of work:** Division of work and specialization produces more and better work with the same effort.

- **Authority and responsibility:** Authority is the right to give orders and the power to exact obedience. A manager has official authority because of her position, as well as personal authority based on individual personality, intelligence, and experience. Authority creates responsibility.

- **Discipline:** Obedience and respect within an organization are absolutely essential. Good discipline requires managers to apply sanctions whenever violations become apparent.

- **Unity of command:** An employee should receive orders from only one superior.

- **Unity of direction:** Organizational activities must have one central authority and one plan of action.

- **Subordination of individual interest to general interest:** The interests of one employee or group of employees are subordinate to the interests and goals of the organization.

- **Remuneration of personnel:** Salaries — the price of services rendered by employees — should be fair and provide satisfaction both to the employee and employer.

- **Centralization:** The objective of centralization is the best utilization of personnel. The degree of centralization varies according to the dynamics of each organization.

- **Scalar chain:** A chain of authority exists from the highest organizational authority to the lowest ranks.

- **Order:** Organizational order for materials and personnel is essential. The right materials and the right employees are necessary for each organizational function and activity.

- **Equity:** In organizations, equity is a combination of kindliness and justice. Both equity and equality of treatment should be considered when dealing with employees.

- **Stability of tenure of personnel:** To attain the maximum productivity of personnel, a stable work force is needed.

- **Initiative:** Thinking out a plan and ensuring its success is an extremely strong motivator. Zeal, energy, and initiative are desired at all levels of the organizational ladder.

■ **Esprit de corps:** Teamwork is fundamentally important to an organization. Work teams and extensive face-to-face verbal communication encourages teamwork.

Mary Parker Follett stressed the importance of an organization establishing common goals for its employees. However, she also began to think somewhat differently than the other theorists of her day, discarding command-style hierarchical organizations where employees were treated like robots. She began to talk about such things as ethics, power, and leadership. She encouraged managers to allow employees to participate in decision making. She stressed the importance of people rather than techniques — a concept very much before her time. As a result, she was a pioneer and often not taken seriously by management scholars of her time. But times change, and innovative ideas from the past suddenly take on new meanings. Much of what managers do today is based on the fundamentals that Follett established more than 70 years ago.

Chester Barnard, who was president of New Jersey Bell Telephone Company, introduced the idea of the **informal organization** — *cliques* (exclusive groups of people) that naturally form within a company. He felt that these informal organizations provided necessary and vital communication functions for the overall organization and that they could help the organization accomplish its goals.

Barnard felt that it was particularly important for managers to develop a sense of common purpose where a willingness to cooperate is strongly encouraged. He is credited with developing the **acceptance theory of management,** which emphasizes the willingness of employees to accept that mangers have legitimate authority to act. Barnard felt that four factors affected the willingness of employees to accept authority:

■ The employees must understand the communication.

■ The employees accept the communication as being consistent with the organization's purposes.

■ The employees feel that their actions will be consistent with the needs and desires of the other employees.

■ The employees feel that they are mentally and physically able to carry out the order.

Barnard's sympathy for and understanding of employee needs positioned him as a bridge to the behavioral school of management, the next school of thought to emerge.

Behavioral Management Theory

As management research continued in the 20th century, questions began to come up regarding the interactions and motivations of the individual within organizations. Management principles developed during the classical period were simply not useful in dealing with many management situations and could not explain the behavior of individual employees. In short, classical theory ignored employee motivation and behavior. As a result, the behavioral school was a natural outgrowth of this revolutionary management experiment.

The **behavioral management theory** is often called the human relations movement because it addresses the human dimension of work. Behavioral theorists believed that a better understanding of human behavior at work, such as motivation, conflict, expectations, and group dynamics, improved productivity.

The theorists who contributed to this school viewed employees as individuals, resources, and assets to be developed and worked with — not as machines, as in the past. Several individuals and experiments contributed to this theory.

Elton Mayo's contributions came as part of the *Hawthorne studies,* a series of experiments that rigorously applied classical management theory only to reveal its shortcomings. The Hawthorne experiments consisted of two studies conducted at the Hawthorne Works of the Western Electric Company in Chicago from 1924 to 1932. The first study was conducted by a group of engineers seeking to determine the relationship of lighting levels to worker productivity. Surprisingly enough, they discovered that worker productivity increased as the lighting levels decreased — that is, until the employees were unable to see what they were doing, after which performance naturally declined.

A few years later, a second group of experiments began. Harvard researchers Mayo and F. J. Roethlisberger supervised a group of five women in a bank wiring room. They gave the women special privileges, such as the right to leave their workstations without permission, take rest periods, enjoy free lunches, and have variations in pay levels and workdays. This experiment also resulted in significantly increased rates of productivity.

In this case, Mayo and Roethlisberger concluded that the increase in productivity resulted from the supervisory arrangement rather than the changes in lighting or other associated worker benefits. Because the experimenters became the primary supervisors of the employees, the intense interest they displayed for the workers was the basis for the increased motivation and resulting productivity. Essentially, the experimenters became a part of the study and influenced its outcome. This is the origin of the term *Hawthorne effect,* which describes the special attention researchers give to a study's subjects and the impact that attention has on the study's findings.

The general conclusion from the Hawthorne studies was that human relations and the social needs of workers are crucial aspects of business management. This principle of human motivation helped revolutionize theories and practices of management.

Abraham Maslow, a practicing psychologist, developed one of the most widely recognized **need theories,** a theory of motivation based upon a consideration of human needs. His theory of human needs had three assumptions:

- Human needs are never completely satisfied.

- Human behavior is purposeful and is motivated by the need for satisfaction.

- Needs can be classified according to a hierarchical structure of importance, from the lowest to highest.

Maslow broke down the needs hierarchy into five specific areas:

- **Physiological needs.** Maslow grouped all physical needs necessary for maintaining basic human well-being, such as food and drink, into this category. After the need is satisfied, however, it is no longer is a motivator.

- **Safety needs.** These needs include the need for basic security, stability, protection, and freedom from fear. A normal state exists for an individual to have all these needs generally satisfied. Otherwise, they become primary motivators.

- **Belonging and love needs.** After the physical and safety needs are satisfied and are no longer motivators, the need for belonging and love emerges as a primary motivator. The individual strives to establish meaningful relationships with significant others.

- **Esteem needs.** An individual must develop self-confidence and wants to achieve status, reputation, fame, and glory.

- **Self-actualization needs.** Assuming that all the previous needs in the hierarchy are satisfied, an individual feels a need to find himself.

Maslow's hierarchy of needs theory helped managers visualize employee motivation. For more on this theory, see Chapter 11.

Douglas McGregor was heavily influenced by both the Hawthorne studies and Maslow. He believed that two basic kinds of managers exist. One type, the Theory X manager, has a negative view of employees and assumes that they are lazy, untrustworthy, and incapable of assuming responsibility. On the other hand, the Theory Y manager assumes that employees are not only trustworthy and capable of assuming responsibility, but also have high levels of motivation.

An important aspect of McGregor's idea was his belief that managers who hold either set of assumptions can create **self-fulfilling prophecies** — that through their behavior, these managers create situations where subordinates act in ways that confirm the manager's original expectations.

As a group, these theorists discovered that people worked for inner satisfaction and not materialistic rewards, shifting the focus to the role of individuals in an organization's performance.

Quantitative School of Management

During World War II, mathematicians, physicists, and other scientists joined together to solve military problems. The quantitative school of management is a result of the research conducted during World War II. The **quantitative approach** to management involves the use of quantitative techniques, such as statistics, information models, and computer simulations, to improve decision making. This school consists of several branches, described in the following sections.

Management science

The management science school emerged to treat the problems associated with global warfare. Today, this view encourages managers to use mathematics, statistics, and other quantitative techniques to make management decisions.

Managers can use computer models to figure out the best way to do something — saving both money and time. Managers use several science applications.

- Mathematical forecasting helps make projections that are useful in the planning process.

- Inventory modeling helps control inventories by mathematically establishing how and when to order a product.

- Queuing theory helps allocate service personnel or workstations to minimize customer waiting and service cost.

Operations management

Operations management is a narrow branch of the quantitative approach to management. It focuses on managing the process of transforming materials, labor, and capital into useful goods and/or services. The product outputs can be either goods or services; effective operations management is a concern for both manufacturing and service organizations. The resource inputs, or factors of production, include the wide variety of raw materials, technologies, capital information, and people needed to create finished products. The transformation process, in turn, is the actual set of operations or activities through which various resources are utilized to produce finished goods or services of value to customers or clients.

Operations management today pays close attention to the demands of quality, customer service, and competition. The process begins with attention to the needs of customers: What do they want? Where do they want it? When do they want it? Based on the answers to these questions, managers line up resources and take any action necessary to meet customer expectations.

Management information systems

Management information systems (MIS) is the most recent subfield of the quantitative school. A management information system organizes past, present, and projected data from both internal and external sources and processes it into usable information, which it then makes available to managers at all organizational levels. The information systems are also able to organize data into usable and accessible formats. As a result, managers can identify alternatives quickly, evaluate alternatives by using a spreadsheet program, pose a series of "what-if" questions, and finally, select the best alternatives based on the answers to these questions.

Systems management theory

The **systems management theory** has had a significant effect on management science. A system is an interrelated set of elements functioning as a whole. An organization as a system is composed of four elements:

- **Inputs** — material or human resources
- **Transformation processes** — technological and managerial processes
- **Outputs** — products or services
- **Feedback** — reactions from the environment

In relationship to an organization, *inputs* include resources such as raw materials, money, technologies, and people. These inputs go through a transformation process where they're planned, organized, motivated, and controlled to ultimately meet the organization's goals. The *outputs* are the products or services designed to enhance the quality of life or productivity for customers/clients. Feedback includes comments from customers or clients using the products. This overall systems framework applies to any department or program in the overall organization.

Systems theory may seem quite basic. Yet decades of management training and practices in the workplace have not followed this theory. Only recently, with tremendous changes facing organizations and how they operate, have educators and managers come to face this new way of looking at things. This interpretation has brought about a significant change in the way management studies and approaches organizations.

The systems theory encourages managers to look at the organization from a broader perspective. Managers are beginning to recognize the various parts of the organization, and, in particular, the interrelations of the parts.

Contemporary system theorists find it helpful to analyze the effectiveness of organizations according to the degree that they are open or closed. The following terminology is important to your understanding of the systems approach:

- An organization that interacts little with its external environment (outside environment) and therefore receives little feedback from it is called a **closed system.**

- An **open system,** in contrast, interacts continually with its environment. Therefore, it is well informed about changes within its surroundings and its position relative to these changes.

- A **subsystem** is any system that is part of a larger one.

- **Entropy** is the tendency of systems to deteriorate or break down over time.

- **Synergy** is the ability of the whole system to equal more than the sum of its parts.

Contingency School of Management

The contingency school of management can be summarized as an "it all depends" approach. The appropriate management actions and approaches depend on the situation. Managers with a contingency view use a flexible approach, draw on a variety of theories and experiences, and evaluate many options as they solve problems.

Contingency management recognizes that there is no one best way to manage. In the contingency perspective, managers are faced with the task of determining which managerial approach is likely to be most effective in a given situation. For example, the approach used to manage a group of teenagers working in a fast-food restaurant would be very different from the approach used to manage a medical research team trying to find a cure for a disease.

Contingency thinking avoids the classical "one best way" arguments and recognizes the need to understand situational differences and respond appropriately to them. It does not apply certain management principles to any situation. Contingency theory is a recognition of the extreme importance of individual manager performance in any given situation. The contingency approach is highly dependent on the experience and judgment of the manager in a given organizational environment.

Quality School of Management

The quality school of management is a comprehensive concept for leading and operating an organization, aimed at continually improving performance by focusing on customers while addressing the needs of all stakeholders. In other words, this concept focuses on managing the total organization to deliver high quality to customers.

The quality school of management considers the following in its theory:

- **Organization makeup.** Organizations are made up of complex systems of customers and suppliers. Every individual, executive, manager, and worker functions as both a supplier and a customer.

- **Quality of goods and services.** Meeting the customers' requirements is a priority goal and presumed to be a key to organizational survival and growth.

- **Continuous improvement in goods and services.** Recognizing the need to pinpoint internal and external requirements and continuously strive to improve. It is an idea that says, "the company is good, but it can always become better."

- **Employees working in teams.** These groups are primary vehicles for planning and problem solving.

- **Developing openness and trust.** Confidence among members of the organization at all levels is an important condition for success.

Quality management involves employees in decision making as a way to prevent quality problems. The **Kaizen** (pronounced *ky*-zen) approach uses incremental, continuous improvement for people, products, and processes. The reengineering approach focuses on sensing the need to change, seeing change coming, and reacting effectively to it when it comes. Both approaches are described in the following sections.

Kaizen approach

The very notion of continuous improvement suggests that managers, teams, and individuals learn from both their accomplishments and their mistakes. Quality managers help their employees gain insights from personal work experiences, and they encourage everyone to share with others what they have learned. In this way, everyone reflects upon his or her own work experiences, including failures, and passes their newfound knowledge to others. Sharing experiences in this manner helps to create an organization that is continuously discovering new ways to improve.

Kaizen is the commitment to work toward steady, continual improvement. The best support for continuous improvement is an organization of people who give a high priority to learning. In this process, everyone in the organization participates by identifying opportunities for improvement, testing new approaches, recording the results, and recommending changes.

Reengineering approach

The reengineering approach to management focuses on creating change — big change — and fast. It centers on sensing the need to change, seeing change coming, and reacting effectively to change when it comes.

Reengineering — the radical redesign of business processes to achieve dramatic improvements in cost, quality, service, and speed — requires that every employee and manager look at all aspects of the company's operation and find ways to rebuild the organizational systems to improve efficiency, identify redundancies, and eliminate waste in every possible way. Reengineering is neither easy nor cheap, but companies that adopt this plan have reaped remarkable results.

Reengineering efforts look at how jobs are designed, and raise critical questions about how much work and work processes can be optimally configured. Although many people believe that reengineering is a euphemism for downsizing or outsourcing, this is not true. Yes, downsizing or outsourcing may be a byproduct of reengineering. However, the goal of reengineering is to bring about a tight fit between market opportunities and corporate abilities. After organizations are able to find this fit, new jobs should be created.

Management in the Future

Modern management approaches respect the classical, human resource, and quantitative approaches to management. However, successful managers recognize that although each theoretical school has limitations in its applications, each approach also offers valuable insights that can broaden a manager's options in solving problems and achieving organizational goals. Successful managers work to extend these approaches to meet the demands of a dynamic environment.

Modern management approaches recognize that people are complex and variable. Employee needs change over time; people possess a range of talents and capabilities that can be developed. Organizations and managers, therefore, should respond to individuals with a wide variety of managerial strategies and job opportunities.

Key themes to be considered, as the twenty-first century progresses, include the following:

- The commitment to meet customer needs 100 percent of the time guides organizations toward quality management and continuous improvement of operations.

- Today's global economy is a dramatic influence on organizations, and opportunities abound to learn new ways of managing from practices in other countries.

- Organizations must reinvest in their most important asset, their people. If organizations cannot make the commitment to lifelong employment, they must commit to using attrition to reduce head count. They will not receive cooperation unless they make it clear that their people will not be working themselves out of a job.

- Managers must excel in their leadership responsibilities to perform numerous different roles.

Chapter Checkout

Q&A

1. Classical management thinkers _____.
   a. utilize the "it all depends" approach
   b. utilize quantitative decision-making tools
   c. look for the one best way to do something
   d. realize that their most important and complex resource is people

2. The Hawthorne studies are an important foundation of the _____ approaches.
   a. classical
   b. human relations
   c. administrative
   d. quantitative

3. Models, simulations, and queuing theory are examples of techniques found in the _____ approach to management.
   a. classical
   b. quantitative
   c. bureaucratic organization
   d. modern

4. Which of the following statements does *not* accurately reflect the characteristics of contingency theory?
   a. Managers should draw on all past theories in attempting to analyze and solve problems.
   b. The best way to initially approach all management problems is through scientific management.
   c. The contingency approach is integrative in nature.
   d. Managers should stay flexible and consider the alternatives and fallback positions when defining and attacking problems.

5. In a fast-changing environment, the most effective method of improving the quality of a product would be _____.
   a. Kaizen
   b. bureaucracy
   c. reengineering
   d. management science

Answers: 1. c **2.** b **3.** b **4.** b **5.** c

Chapter 3

MANAGERIAL ENVIRONMENTS

Chapter Check-In

❑ Identifying environments that impact organizations

❑ Understanding external factors that influence managers' roles

❑ Interpreting internal factors that affect managerial duties

❑ Learning why an organization must adapt to the environment

A manager's environment is made up of constantly changing factors — both external and internal — that affect the operation of the organization. If a new competitor appears in the marketplace, the managerial environment is affected. If key clients take their business elsewhere, managers feel the impact. And if technological advances date an organization's current methods of doing business, once again, the managerial environment has to adapt.

Although managers can't always control their environments, they need to be aware of any changes that occur, because changes ultimately affect their daily decisions and actions. For example, in the airline industry, deregulation opened up the market to new airlines, forcing existing airlines to be more competitive. Managers in existing airlines couldn't afford to ignore the cheaper airfares and increased service that resulted. Not only did managers have to identify the new challenge, but they also had to act quickly and efficiently to remain competitive.

In this chapter, the two types of environments that affect management and how organizations adapt to them are discussed.

The External Environment

All outside factors that may affect an organization make up the external environment. The external environment is divided into two parts:

- **Directly interactive:** This environment has an immediate and first-hand impact upon the organization. A new competitor entering the market is an example.

- **Indirectly interactive:** This environment has a secondary and more distant effect upon the organization. New legislation taking effect may have a great impact. For example, complying with the Americans with Disabilities Act requires employers to update their facilities to accommodate those with disabilities.

The following sections describe these two forces in more detail.

Directly interactive forces

Directly interactive forces include owners, customers, suppliers, competitors, employees, and employee unions. Management has a responsibility to each of these groups. Here are some examples:

- **Owners** expect managers to watch over their interests and provide a return on investments.

- **Customers** demand satisfaction with the products and services they purchase and use.

- **Suppliers** require attentive communication, payment, and a strong working relationship to provide needed resources.

- **Competitors** present challenges as they vie for customers in a marketplace with similar products or services.

- **Employees and employee unions** provide both the people to do the jobs and the representation of work force concerns to management.

Indirectly interactive forces

The second type of external environment is the *indirectly interactive* forces. These forces include sociocultural, political and legal, technological, economic, and global influences. Indirectly interactive forces may impact one organization more than another simply because of the nature of a particular business. For example, a company that relies heavily on technology will be more affected by software updates than a company that uses just one computer. Although somewhat removed, indirect forces are still important to the interactive nature of an organization.

The *sociocultural* dimension is especially important because it determines the goods, services, and standards that society values. The sociocultural force includes the demographics and values of a particular customer base.

- **Demographics** are measures of the various characteristics of the people and social groups who make up a society. Age, gender, and income are examples of commonly used demographic characteristics.

- **Values** refer to certain beliefs that people have about different forms of behavior or products. Changes in how a society values an item or a behavior can greatly affect a business. (Think of all the fads that have come and gone!)

The *political and legal dimensions* of the external environment include regulatory parameters within which an organization must operate. Political parties create or influence laws, and business owners must abide by these laws. Tax policies, trade regulations, and minimum wage legislation are just a few examples of political and legal issues that may affect the way an organization operates.

The *technological dimension* of the external environment impacts the scientific processes used in changing inputs (resources, labor, money) to outputs (goods and services). The success of many organizations depends on how well they identify and respond to external technological changes.

For example, one of the most significant technological dimensions of the last several decades has been the increasing availability and affordability of management information systems (also known as MIS; see Chapter 2 for more information). Through these systems, managers have access to information that can improve the way they operate and manage their businesses.

The *economic dimension* reflects worldwide financial conditions. Certain economic conditions of special concern to organizations include interest rates, inflation, unemployment rates, gross national product, and the value of the U.S. dollar against other currencies.

A favorable economic climate generally represents opportunities for growth in many industries, such as sales of clothing, jewelry, and new cars. But some businesses traditionally benefit in poor economic conditions. The alcoholic beverage industry, for example, traditionally fares well during times of economic downturn.

The *global dimension* of the environment refers to factors in other countries that affect U.S. organizations. Although the basic management functions of planning, organizing, staffing, leading, and controlling are the same whether a company operates domestically or internationally, managers encounter difficulties and risks on an international scale. Whether it be unfamiliarity with language or customs, or a problem within the country itself (think mad cow disease), managers encounter global risks that they probably wouldn't have encountered if they had stayed on their own shores.

The Internal Environment

An organization's *internal environment* is composed of the elements within the organization, including current employees, management, and especially corporate culture, which defines employee behavior. Although some elements affect the organization as a whole, others affect only the manager. A manager's philosophical or leadership style directly impacts employees. Traditional managers give explicit instructions to employees, while progressive managers empower employees to make many of their own decisions. Changes in philosophy and/or leadership style are under the control of the manager. The following sections describe some of the elements that make up the internal environment.

Organizational mission statements

An organization's **mission statement** describes what the organization stands for and why it exists. It explains the overall purpose of the organization and includes the attributes that distinguish it from other organizations of its type.

A mission statement should be more than words on a piece of paper; it should reveal a company's philosophy, as well as its purpose. This declaration should be a living, breathing document that provides information and inspiration for the members of the organization. A mission statement should answer the questions, "What are our values?" and "What do we stand for?" This statement provides focus for an organization by rallying its members to work together to achieve its common goals.

But not all mission statements are effective in America's businesses. Effective mission statements lead to effective efforts. In today's quality-conscious and highly competitive environments, an effective mission statement's purpose is centered on serving the needs of customers. A good mission statement is precise in identifying the following intents of a company:

- **Customers** — who will be served
- **Products/services** — what will be produced
- **Location** — where the products/services will be produced
- **Philosophy** — what ideology will be followed

Company policies

Company policies are guidelines that govern how certain organizational situations are addressed. Just as colleges maintain policies about admittance, grade appeals, prerequisites, and waivers, companies establish policies to provide guidance to managers who must make decisions about circumstances that occur frequently within their organization. Company policies are an indication of an organization's personality and should coincide with its mission statement.

Formal structures

The **formal structure** of an organization is the hierarchical arrangement of tasks and people. This structure determines how information flows within the organization, which departments are responsible for which activities, and where the decision-making power rests.

Some organizations use a chart to simplify the breakdown of its formal structure. This **organizational chart** is a pictorial display of the official lines of authority and communication within an organization. (Chapter 6 describes the organizing function, and Chapter 7 offers examples of organizational charts.)

Organizational cultures

The **organizational culture** is an organization's personality. Just as each reader of this book has a distinct personality, so does each organization. The culture of an organization distinguishes it from others and shapes the actions of its members.

Four main components make up an organization's culture:

- Values
- Heroes
- Rites and rituals
- Social network

Values are the basic beliefs that define employees' successes in an organization. For example, many universities place high values on professors being published. If a faculty member is published in a professional journal, for example, his or her chances of receiving tenure may be enhanced. The university wants to ensure that a published professor stays with the university for the duration of his or her academic career — and this professor's ability to write for publications is a value.

The second component is heroes. A *hero* is an exemplary person who reflects the image, attitudes, or values of the organization and serves as a role model to other employees. A hero is sometimes the founder of the organization (think Sam Walton of Wal-Mart). However, the hero of a company doesn't have to be the founder; it can be an everyday worker, such as hard-working paralegal Erin Brockovich, who had a tremendous impact on the organization.

Rites and rituals, the third component, are routines or ceremonies that the company uses to recognize high-performing employees. Awards banquets, company gatherings, and quarterly meetings can acknowledge distinguished employees for outstanding service. The honorees are meant to exemplify and inspire all employees of the company during the rest of the year.

The final component, the *social network,* is the informal means of communication within an organization. This network, sometimes referred to as the company grapevine, carries the stories of both heroes and those who have failed. It is through this network that employees really learn about the organization's culture and values.

Organizational climates

A byproduct of the company's culture is the **organizational climate.** The overall tone of the workplace and the morale of its workers are elements of daily climate. Worker attitudes dictate the positive or negative "atmosphere" of the workplace. The daily relationships and interactions of employees are indicative of an organization's climate.

Resources

Resources are the people, information, facilities, infrastructure, machinery, equipment, supplies, and finances at an organization's disposal. People are the paramount resource of all organizations. Information, facilities, machinery equipment, materials, supplies, and finances are supporting, nonhuman resources that complement workers in their quests to accomplish the organization's mission statement. The availability of resources and the way that managers value the human and nonhuman resources impact the organization's environment.

Managerial philosophies

Philosophy of management is the manager's set of personal beliefs and values about people and work and as such, is something that the manager can control. As outlined in Chapter 2, McGregor emphasized that a manager's philosophy creates a self-fulfilling prophecy. Theory X managers treat employees almost as children who need constant direction, while Theory Y managers treat employees as competent adults capable of participating in work-related decisions. These managerial philosophies then have a subsequent effect on employee behavior, leading to the self-fulfilling prophecy. As a result, organizational philosophies and managerial philosophies need to be in harmony.

Managerial leadership styles

The number of coworkers involved within a problem-solving or decision-making process reflects the manager's *leadership style*. *Empowerment* means delegating to subordinates decision-making authority, freedom, knowledge, autonomy, and skills. Fortunately, most organizations and managers are making the move toward the active participation and teamwork that empowerment entails.

When guided properly, an empowered workforce may lead to heightened productivity and quality, reduced costs, more innovation, improved customer service, and greater commitment from the employees of the organization. In addition, response time may improve, because information and decisions need not be passed up and down the hierarchy. Empowering employees makes good sense because employees closest to the actual problem to be solved or the customer to be served can make the necessary decisions more easily than a supervisor or manager removed from the scene.

Adapting to Environments

The role of a manager is to monitor and shape the internal and external environments and to anticipate changes and react quickly to them.

Managers can monitor the environments through **boundary spanning** — a process of gathering information about developments that could impact the future of the organization. Managers can access information through a variety of sources: customer and supplier feedback; professional, trade, and government publications; industry associations; and personal contacts.

Managers can also actively work to influence their external environments through lobbying, voting, and using the media to influence public opinion.

Internal elements comprise the organization itself. Internal change arises from activities and decisions within the organization. Managers can gather information by conducting a thorough evaluation of the internal operations of the organization. The purpose of this internal analysis is to identify the organizational assets, resources, skills, and processes that represent either strengths or weaknesses. Strengths are aspects of the organization's operations that represent potential **competitive advantages** (any aspect of an organization that distinguishes it from its competitors in a postive way), while weaknesses are areas that are in need of improvement.

Several key areas of the organization's operations should be examined in an internal analysis. Key areas to be assessed include the marketing, financial, research and development, production, and general management capabilities. These areas are typically evaluated in terms of the extents to which they foster quality and support the competitive advantage sought by the organization.

Chapter Checkout

Q&A

1. An organization that regularly affects and is affected by various and constantly changing forces can be described as a(n) _____.
   a. natural force
   b. sociocultural force
   c. open system
   d. closed system

2. Of the following, which is a directly interactive force in an organization's external environment?
   a. technological forces
   b. leadership
   c. economic forces
   d. customers

3. Which of the following is not an indirectly interactive force in an organization's external environment?
   a. sociocultural forces
   b. competitive forces
   c. legal/political forces
   d. technological forces

4. The term organizational climate defines _____.
   a. how the employees feel about working for the organization
   b. how organizations share values, beliefs, habits, norms, philosophies, experiences, and behaviors
   c. what the company does best
   d. a key concept that guides managers and their actions

5. Boundary spanning sources include all of the following except _____.

   a. customers

   b. competitors

   c. government statistics

   d. core values

Answers: 1. c **2.** d **3.** b **4.** a **5.** a

Chapter 4

DECISION MAKING AND PROBLEM SOLVING

Chapter Check-In

❑ Breaking down the decision-making process

❑ Recognizing the factors that influence managerial decisions

❑ Identifying individual problem-solving styles

❑ Becoming familiar with quantitative tools that assist decision makers

Quite literally, organizations operate by people making decisions. A manager plans, organizes, staffs, leads, and controls her team by executing decisions. The effectiveness and quality of those decisions determine how successful a manager will be.

In this chapter, the decision-making process is discussed — from defining the problem to implementing the decision. In addition, the topic of tools that can help managers during the decision-making process is also examined.

The Decision-Making Process

Managers are constantly called upon to make decisions in order to solve problems. Decision making and problem solving are ongoing processes of evaluating situations or problems, considering alternatives, making choices, and following them up with the necessary actions. Sometimes the decision-making process is extremely short, and mental reflection is essentially instantaneous. In other situations, the process can drag on for weeks or even months. The entire decision-making process is dependent upon the right information being available to the right people at the right times.

The decision-making process involves the following steps:

1. Define the problem.
2. Identify limiting factors.
3. Develop potential alternatives.
4. Analyze the alternatives.
5. Select the best alternative.
6. Implement the decision.
7. Establish a control and evaluation system.

Define the problem

The decision-making process begins when a manager identifies the real problem. The accurate definition of the problem affects all the steps that follow; if the problem is inaccurately defined, every step in the decision-making process will be based on an incorrect starting point. One way that a manager can help determine the true problem in a situation is by identifying the problem separately from its symptoms.

The most obviously troubling situations found in an organization can usually be identified as symptoms of underlying problems. (See Table 4-1 for some examples of symptoms.) These symptoms all indicate that something is wrong with an organization, but they don't identify root causes. A successful manager doesn't just attack symptoms; he works to uncover the factors that cause these symptoms.

Table 4-1   Symptoms and Their Real Causes

Symptoms	Underlying Problem
Low profits and/or declining sales	Poor market research
High costs	Poor design process; poorly trained employees
Low morale	Lack of communication between management and subordinates
High employee turnover	Rate of pay too low; job design not suitable
High rate of absenteeism	Employees believe that they are not valued

Identify limiting factors

All managers want to make the best decisions. To do so, managers need to have the ideal resources — information, time, personnel, equipment, and supplies — and identify any limiting factors. Realistically, managers operate in an environment that normally doesn't provide ideal resources. For example, they may lack the proper budget or may not have the most accurate information or any extra time. So, they must choose to **satisfice** — to make the best decision possible with the information, resources, and time available.

Develop potential alternatives

Time pressures frequently cause a manager to move forward after considering only the first or most obvious answers. However, successful problem solving requires thorough examination of the challenge, and a quick answer may not result in a permanent solution. Thus, a manager should think through and investigate several alternative solutions to a single problem before making a quick decision.

One of the best known methods for developing alternatives is through **brainstorming,** where a group works together to generate ideas and alternative solutions. The assumption behind brainstorming is that the group dynamic stimulates thinking — one person's ideas, no matter how outrageous, can generate ideas from the others in the group. Ideally, this spawning of ideas is contagious, and before long, lots of suggestions and ideas flow. Brainstorming usually requires 30 minutes to an hour. The following specific rules should be followed during brainstorming sessions:

- **Concentrate on the problem at hand.** This rule keeps the discussion very specific and avoids the group's tendency to address the events leading up to the current problem.

- **Entertain all ideas.** In fact, the more ideas that come up, the better. In other words, there are no bad ideas. Encouragement of the group to freely offer all thoughts on the subject is important. Participants should be encouraged to present ideas no matter how ridiculous they seem, because such ideas may spark a creative thought on the part of someone else.

- **Refrain from allowing members to evaluate others' ideas on the spot.** All judgments should be deferred until all thoughts are presented, and the group concurs on the best ideas.

Although brainstorming is the most common technique to develop alternative solutions, managers can use several other ways to help develop solutions. Here are some examples:

- **Nominal group technique.** This method involves the use of a highly structured meeting, complete with an agenda, and restricts discussion or interpersonal communication during the decision-making process. This technique is useful because it ensures that every group member has equal input in the decision-making process. It also avoids some of the pitfalls, such as pressure to conform, group dominance, hostility, and conflict, that can plague a more interactive, spontaneous, unstructured forum such as brainstorming.

- **Delphi technique.** With this technique, participants never meet, but a group leader uses written questionnaires to conduct the decision making.

No matter what technique is used, group decision making has clear advantages and disadvantages when compared with individual decision making. The following are among the advantages:

- Groups provide a broader perspective.

- Employees are more likely to be satisfied and to support the final decision.

- Opportunities for discussion help to answer questions and reduce uncertainties for the decision makers.

These points are among the disadvantages:

- This method can be more time-consuming than one individual making the decision on his own.

- The decision reached could be a compromise rather than the optimal solution.

- Individuals become guilty of *groupthink* — the tendency of members of a group to conform to the prevailing opinions of the group.

- Groups may have difficulty performing tasks because the group, rather than a single individual, makes the decision, resulting in confusion when it comes time to implement and evaluate the decision.

The results of dozens of individual-versus-group performance studies indicate that groups not only tend to make better decisions than a person acting alone, but also that groups tend to inspire star performers to even higher levels of productivity.

So, are two (or more) heads better than one? The answer depends on several factors, such as the nature of the task, the abilities of the group members, and the form of interaction. Because a manager often has a choice between making a decision independently or including others in the decision making, she needs to understand the advantages and disadvantages of group decision making.

Analyze the alternatives

The purpose of this step is to decide the relative merits of each idea. Managers must identify the advantages and disadvantages of each alternative solution before making a final decision.

Evaluating the alternatives can be done in numerous ways. Here are a few possibilities:

- Determine the pros and cons of each alternative.

- Perform a cost-benefit analysis for each alternative.

- Weight each factor important in the decision, ranking each alternative relative to its ability to meet each factor, and then multiply by a probability factor to provide a final value for each alternative.

Regardless of the method used, a manager needs to evaluate each alternative in terms of its

- **Feasibility** — Can it be done?

- **Effectiveness** — How well does it resolve the problem situation?

- **Consequences** — What will be its costs (financial and nonfinancial) to the organization?

Select the best alternative

After a manager has analyzed all the alternatives, she must decide on the best one. The best alternative is the one that produces the most advantages and the fewest serious disadvantages. Sometimes, the selection process can be fairly straightforward, such as the alternative with the most pros and fewest cons. Other times, the optimal solution is a combination of several alternatives.

Sometimes, though, the best alternative may not be obvious. That's when a manager must decide which alternative is the most feasible and effective, coupled with which carries the lowest costs to the organization. (See the preceding section.) Probability estimates, where analysis of each alternative's chances of success takes place, often come into play at this point in the decision-making process. In those cases, a manager simply selects the alternative with the highest probability of success.

Implement the decision

Managers are paid to make decisions, but they are also paid to get results from these decisions. Positive results must follow decisions. Everyone involved with the decision must know his or her role in ensuring a successful outcome. To make certain that employees understand their roles, managers must thoughtfully devise programs, procedures, rules, or policies to help aid them in the problem-solving process.

Establish a control and evaluation system

Ongoing actions need to be monitored. An evaluation system should provide feedback on how well the decision is being implemented, what the results are, and what adjustments are necessary to get the results that were intended when the solution was chosen.

In order for a manager to evaluate his decision, he needs to gather information to determine its effectiveness. Was the original problem resolved? If not, is he closer to the desired situation than he was at the beginning of the decision-making process?

If a manager's plan hasn't resolved the problem, he needs to figure out what went wrong. A manager may accomplish this by asking the following questions:

- **Was the wrong alternative selected?** If so, one of the other alternatives generated in the decision-making process may be a wiser choice.

- **Was the correct alternative selected, but implemented improperly?** If so, a manager should focus attention solely on the implementation step to ensure that the chosen alternative is implemented successfully.

- **Was the original problem identified incorrectly?** If so, the decision-making process needs to begin again, starting with a revised identification step.

■ **Has the implemented alternative been given enough time to be successful?** If not, a manager should give the process more time and re-evaluate at a later date.

Conditions That Influence Decison Making

Managers make problem-solving decisions under three different conditions: certainty, risk, and uncertainty. All managers make decisions under each condition, but risk and uncertainty are common to the more complex and unstructured problems faced by top managers.

Certainty

Decisions are made under the condition of certainty when the manager has perfect knowledge of all the information needed to make a decision. This condition is ideal for problem solving. The challenge is simply to study the alternatives and choose the best solution.

When problems tend to arise on a regular basis, a manager may address them through standard or prepared responses called programmed decisions. These solutions are already available from past experiences and are appropriate for the problem at hand. A good example is the decision to reorder inventory automatically when stock falls below a determined level. Today, an increasing number of programmed decisions are being assisted or handled by computers using decision-support software.

Structured problems are familiar, straightforward, and clear with respect to the information needed to resolve them. A manager can often anticipate these problems and plan to prevent or solve them. For example, personnel problems are common in regard to pay raises, promotions, vacation requests, and committee assignments, as examples. Proactive managers can plan processes for handling these complaints effectively before they even occur.

Risk

In a risk environment, the manager lacks complete information. This condition is more difficult. A manager may understand the problem and the alternatives, but has no guarantee how each solution will work. Risk is a fairly common decision condition for managers.

When new and unfamiliar problems arise, nonprogrammed decisions are specifically tailored to the situations at hand. The information requirements for defining and resolving nonroutine problems are typically high. Although computer support may assist in information processing, the decision will most likely involve human judgment. Most problems faced by higher-level managers demand nonprogrammed decisions. This fact explains why the demands on a manager's conceptual skills (see Chapter 1 for more information) increase as he or she moves into higher levels of managerial responsibility.

A **crisis problem** is an unexpected problem that can lead to disaster if it's not resolved quickly and appropriately. No organization can avoid crises, and the public is well aware of the immensity of corporate crises in the modern world. The Chernobyl nuclear plant explosion in the former Soviet Union and the *Exxon Valdez* spill of years past are a couple of sensational examples. Managers in more progressive organizations now anticipate that crises, unfortunately, will occur. These managers are installing early-warning crisis information systems and developing crisis management plans to deal with these situations in the best possible ways.

Uncertainty

When information is so poor that managers can't even assign probabilities to the likely outcomes of alternatives, the manager is making a decision in an uncertain environment. This condition is the most difficult for a manager. Decision making under conditions of uncertainty is like being a pioneer entering unexplored territory. Uncertainty forces managers to rely heavily on creativity in solving problems: It requires unique and often totally innovative alternatives to existing processes. Groups are frequently used for problem solving in such situations. In all cases, the responses to uncertainty depend greatly on intuition, educated guesses, and hunches — all of which leave considerable room for error.

These unstructured problems involve ambiguities and information deficiencies and often occur as new or unexpected situations. These problems are most often unanticipated and are addressed reactively as they occur. Unstructured problems require novel solutions. Proactive managers are sometimes able to get a jump on unstructured problems by realizing that a situation is susceptible to problems and then making contingency plans. For example, at the Vanguard Group, executives are tireless in their preparations for a variety of events that could disrupt their mutual fund business. Their biggest fear is an investor panic that overloads their customer service system during a major plunge in the bond or stock markets. In anticipation of this occurrence, the firm has trained accountants, lawyers, and fund managers to staff the telephones if needed.

Personal Decison-Making Styles

Managerial decision making depends on many factors, including the ability to set priorities and time decisions correctly. However, the most important influence on managerial decision making is a manager's personal attributes or his or her own decision-making approach. The three most common decision models are as follows:

- Rational/logical

- Intuitive

- Predisposed

Regardless of the model favored by a manager, understanding personal tendencies and moving toward a more rational model should be the manager's goal. The best decisions are usually a result of a blend of the decision maker's intuition and the rational step-by-step approach. These models are described in the next sections.

Rational/Logical decision model

This approach uses a step-by-step process, similar to the seven-step decision-making process described earlier in this chapter. The rational/logical decision model focuses on facts and reasoning. Reliance is on the steps and decision tools, such as payback analysis, decision tree, and research — all are described later in this chapter.

Through the use of quantitative techniques, rationality, and logic, the manager evaluates the alternatives and selects the best solution to the problem.

Intuitive decision model

The managers who use this approach avoid statistical analysis and logical processes. These managers are "gut" decision makers who rely on their feelings about a situation. This definition could easily lead one to believe that intuitive decision making is irrational or arbitrary. Although intuition refers to decision making without formal analysis or conscious reasoning, it is based on years of managerial practice and experience. These experienced managers identify alternatives quickly without conducting systematic analyses of alternatives and their consequences. When making a decision using intuition, the manager recognizes cues in the situation that are the same as or similar to those in previous situations that he or she has experienced; the cues help the manager to rapidly conduct subconscious analysis. Then a decision is made.

Predisposed decision model

A manager who decides on a solution and then gathers material to support the decision uses the predisposed decision model approach. Decision makers using this approach do not search out all possible alternatives. Rather, they identify and evaluate alternatives only until an acceptable decision is found. Having found a satisfactory alternative, the decision maker stops searching for additional solutions. Other, and potentially better, alternatives may exist, but will not be identified or considered because the first workable solution has been accepted. Therefore, only a fraction of the available alternatives may be considered due to the decision maker's information-processing limitations. A manager with this tendency is likely to ignore critical information and may face the same decision again later.

Quantitative Tools to Assist in Decision Making

Quantitative techniques help a manager improve the overall quality of decision making. These techniques are most commonly used in the rational/logical decision model, but they can apply in any of the other models as well. Among the most common techniques are decision trees, payback analysis, and simulations.

Decision trees

A **decision tree** shows a complete picture of a potential decision and allows a manager to graph alternative decision paths. Decision trees are a useful way to analyze hiring, marketing, investments, equipment purchases, pricing, and similar decisions that involve a progression of smaller decisions. Generally, decision trees are used to evaluate decisions under conditions of risk.

The term decision tree comes from the graphic appearance of the technique that starts with the initial decision shown as the base. The various alternatives, based upon possible future environmental conditions, and the payoffs associated with each of the decisions branch from the trunk.

Decision trees force a manager to be explicit in analyzing conditions associated with future decisions and in determining the outcome of different alternatives. The decision tree is a flexible method. It can be used for many situations in which emphasis can be placed on sequential decisions, the probability of various conditions, or the highlighting of alternatives.

Payback analysis

Payback analysis comes in handy if a manager needs to decide whether to purchase a piece of equipment. Say, for example, that a manager is purchasing cars for a rental car company. Although a less-expensive car may take less time to pay off, some clients may want more luxurious models. To decide which cars to purchase, a manager should consider some factors, such as the expected useful life of the car, its warranty and repair record, its cost of insurance, and, of course, the rental demand for the car. Based on the information gathered, a manager can then rank alternatives based on the cost of each car. A higher-priced car may be more appropriate because of its longer life and customer rental demand. The strategy, of course, is for the manager to choose the alternative that has the quickest payback of the initial cost.

Many individuals use payback analysis when they decide whether they should continue their education. They determine how much courses will cost, how much salary they will earn as a result of each course completed and perhaps, degree earned, and how long it will take to recoup the investment. If the benefits outweigh the costs, the payback is worthwhile.

Simulations

Simulation is a broad term indicating any type of activity that attempts to imitate an existing system or situation in a simplified manner. Simulation is basically model building, in which the simulator is trying to gain understanding by replicating something and then manipulating it by adjusting the variables used to build the model.

Simulations have great potential in decision making. In the basic decision-making steps listed earlier in this chapter, Step 4 is the evaluation of alternatives. If a manager could simulate alternatives and predict their outcomes at this point in the decision process, he or she would eliminate much of the guesswork from decision making.

Chapter Checkout

Q&A

1. A manager's first step in the decision-making process is to _____.

   a. define the problem
   b. identify limiting factors
   c. develop potential alternatives
   d. establish a control and evaluation system

2. When a manager knows what the problem is and what the alternatives are, the manager is making the decision under the condition of _____.

   a. imperfect resources

   b. risk

   c. uncertainty

   d. certainty

3. A quantitative technique for decision making that shows a complete picture of potential alternative decision paths is called _____.

   a. the Delphi technique

   b. a decision tree

   c. brainstorming

   d. payback analysis

4. A group effort of generating alternative ideas that can help a manager solve a problem is called _____.

   a. the Delphi technique

   b. out-of-the box thinking

   c. brainstorming

   d. the nominal group technique

5. All of the following are important strategies that a manager can use to create a more effective decision-making environment except _____.

   a. encourage others to make decisions

   b. be ready to try things

   c. rely solely upon himself or herself

   d. recognize the importance of quality information

Answers: 1. a **2.** b **3.** b **4.** c **5.** c

Chapter 5

ORGANIZATIONAL PLANNING

Chapter Check-In

❑ Recognizing planning as an essential management function

❑ Identifying different types of plans designed to meet organizational goals

❑ Determining and overcoming barriers to planning

Of the five management functions — planning, organizing, staffing, leading and controlling — planning is the most fundamental. All other functions stem from planning. However, planning doesn't always get the attention that it deserves; when it does, many managers discover that the planning process isn't as easy as they thought it would be — or that even the best-laid plans can go awry.

In this chapter, the process of planning and the strategies behind different types of plans are discussed. Topics also include the importance of employee involvement and the significance of goal setting.

Defining Planning

Before a manager can tackle any of the other functions, he or she must first devise a plan. A **plan** is a blueprint for goal achievement that specifies the necessary resource allocations, schedules, tasks, and other actions.

A *goal* is a desired future state that the organization attempts to realize. Goals are important because an organization exists for a purpose, and goals define and state that purpose. Goals specify future ends; plans specify today's means.

The word **planning** incorporates both ideas: It means determining the organization's goals and defining the means for achieving them. Planning allows managers the opportunity to adjust to the environment instead of merely reacting to it. Planning increases the possibility of survival in business by actively anticipating and managing the risks that may occur in the future.

In short, planning is preparing for tomorrow, today. It's the activity that allows managers to determine what they want and how they will achieve it.

Not only does planning provide direction and a unity of purpose for organizations, it also answers six basic questions in regard to any activity:

- What needs to be accomplished?

- When is the deadline?

- Where will this be done?

- Who will be responsible for it?

- How will it get done?

- How much time, energy, and resources are required to accomplish this goal?

Recognizing the Advantages of Planning

The military saying, "If you fail to plan, you plan to fail," is very true. Without a plan, managers are set up to encounter errors, waste, and delays. A plan, on the other hand, helps a manager organize resources and activities efficiently and effectively to achieve goals.

The advantages of planning are numerous. Planning fulfills the following objectives:

- **Gives an organization a sense of direction.** Without plans and goals, organizations merely react to daily occurrences without considering what will happen in the long run. For example, the solution that makes sense in the short term doesn't always make sense in the long term. Plans avoid this drift situation and ensure that short-range efforts will support and harmonize with future goals.

- **Focuses attention on objectives and results.** Plans keep the people who carry them out focused on the anticipated results. In addition, keeping sight of the goal also motivates employees.

- **Establishes a basis for teamwork.** Diverse groups cannot effectively cooperate in joint projects without an integrated plan. Examples are numerous: Plumbers, carpenters, and electricians cannot build a house without blueprints. In addition, military activities require the coordination of Army, Navy, and Air Force units.

■ **Helps anticipate problems and cope with change.** When management plans, it can help forecast future problems and make any necessary changes up front to avoid them. Of course, surprises — such as the 1973 quadrupling of oil prices — can always catch an organization short, but many changes are easier to forecast. Planning for these potential problems helps to minimize mistakes and reduce the "surprises" that inevitably occur.

■ **Provides guidelines for decision making.** Decisions are future-oriented. If management doesn't have any plans for the future, they will have few guidelines for making current decisions. If a company knows that it wants to introduce a new product three years in the future, its management must be mindful of the decisions they make now. Plans help both managers and employees keep their eyes on the big picture.

■ **Serves as a prerequisite to employing all other management functions.** Planning is primary, because without knowing what an organization wants to accomplish, management can't intelligently undertake any of the other basic managerial activities: organizing, staffing, leading, and/or controlling.

Using Plans to Achieve Goals

Planning is a crucial activity, for it designs the map that lays the groundwork for the other functions. The plan itself specifies what should be done, by whom, where, when, and how. All businesses — from the smallest restaurant to the largest multinational corporation — need to develop plans for achieving success. But before an organization can plan a course of action, it must first determine what it wants to achieve. *Objectives*, the end results desired by the organization, are derived from the organization's **mission statement.** The mission statement explains what the organization stands for and why it exists. A strong mission statement symbolizes legitimacy to external audiences, such as investors, customers, and suppliers. Likewise, a strong mission statement allows employees to identify with the overall purpose of the organization and commit to preserving it.

The mission statement is the basis for all goals and plans outlined throughout the organization. Therefore, managers must use effective planning and goal-setting techniques to ensure that internal policies, roles, performances, structures, products, and expenditures are in line with the mission of the organization. (For more on mission statements, see Chapter 3.)

Criteria for effective goals

To make sure that goal setting benefits the organization, managers must adopt certain characteristics and guidelines. The following describes these criteria:

- **Goals must be specific and measurable.** When possible, use quantitative terms, such as increasing profits by 2 percent or decreasing student enrollment by 1 percent, to express goals.

- **Goals should cover key result areas.** Because goals cannot be set for every aspect of employee or organizational performance, managers should identify a few key result areas. These key areas are those activities that contribute most to company performance — for example, customer relations or sales.

- **Goals should be challenging but not too difficult.** When goals are unrealistic, they set employees up for failure and lead to low employee morale. However, if goals are too easy, employees may not feel motivated. Managers must be sure that goals are determined based on existing resources and are not beyond the team's time, equipment, and financial resources.

- **Goals should specify the time period over which they will be achieved.** Deadlines give team members something to work toward and help ensure continued progress. At the same time, managers should set short-term deadlines along the way so that their subordinates are not overwhelmed by one big, seemingly unaccomplishable goal. It would be more appropriate to provide a short term goal such as, "Establish a customer database by June 30."

- **Goals should be linked to rewards.** People who attain goals should be rewarded with something meaningful and related to the goal. Not only will employees feel that their efforts are valued, but they will also have something tangible to motivate them in the future.

Coordination of goals

All the different levels of management should have plans that work together to accomplish the organization's purpose. The plans of the top-, middle-, and first-level managers of an organization should work together to achieve the main goal.

All managers plan basically the same way, but the kinds of plans they develop and the amount of time they spend on planning vary. Here are some examples:

- Top-level managers are concerned with longer time periods and with plans for larger organizational units. Their planning includes developing the mission for the organizational units, the organizational objective, and major policy areas. These goals are called *strategic* goals or objectives.

- Middle-level managers' planning responsibilities center on translating broad objectives of top-level management into more specific goals for work units. These goals are called *tactical* goals or objectives.

- First-level managers are involved in day-to-day plans, such as scheduling work hours, deciding what work will be done and by whom, and developing structures to reach these goals. These goals are called *operational* goals or objectives.

If a first-level manager develops a set of plans that contradicts that of a middle-level manager, conflicts will result. Therefore, all managers must work together when planning their activities and the activities of others.

Detailing Types of Plans

Plans commit individuals, departments, organizations, and the resources of each to specific actions for the future. As the previous section explains, effectively designed organizational goals fit into a hierarchy so that the achievement of goals at low levels permits the attainment of high-level goals. This process is called a **means-ends chain** because low-level goals lead to accomplishment of high-level goals.

Three major types of plans can help managers achieve their organization's goals: strategic, tactical, and operational. Operational plans lead to the achievement of tactical plans, which in turn lead to the attainment of strategic plans. In addition to these three types of plans, managers should also develop a contingency plan in case their original plans fail.

Operational plans

The specific results expected from departments, work groups, and individuals are the **operational goals.** These goals are precise and measurable. "Process 150 sales applications each week" or "Publish 20 books this quarter" are examples of operational goals.

An **operational plan** is one that a manager uses to accomplish his or her job responsibilities. Supervisors, team leaders, and facilitators develop operational plans to support tactical plans (see the next section). Operational plans can be a single-use plan or an ongoing plan.

■ **Single-use plans** apply to activities that do not recur or repeat. A one-time occurrence, such as a special sales program, is a single-use plan because it deals with the who, what, where, how, and how much of an activity. A budget is also a single-use plan because it predicts sources and amounts of income and how much they are used for a specific project.

■ **Continuing or ongoing plans** are usually made once and retain their value over a period of years while undergoing periodic revisions and updates. The following are examples of ongoing plans:

> A **policy** provides a broad guideline for managers to follow when dealing with important areas of decision making. Policies are general statements that explain how a manager should attempt to handle routine management responsibilities. Typical human resources policies, for example, address such matters as employee hiring, terminations, performance appraisals, pay increases, and discipline.

> A **procedure** is a set of step-by-step directions that explains how activities or tasks are to be carried out. Most organizations have procedures for purchasing supplies and equipment, for example. This procedure usually begins with a supervisor completing a purchasing requisition. The requisition is then sent to the next level of management for approval. The approved requisition is forwarded to the purchasing department. Depending on the amount of the request, the purchasing department may place an order, or they may need to secure quotations and/or bids for several vendors before placing the order. By defining the steps to be taken and the order in which they are to be done, procedures provide a standardized way of responding to a repetitive problem.

> A **rule** is an explicit statement that tells an employee what he or she can and cannot do. Rules are "do" and "don't" statements put into place to promote the safety of employees and the uniform treatment and behavior of employees. For example, rules about tardiness and absenteeism permit supervisors to make discipline decisions rapidly and with a high degree of fairness.

Tactical plans

A **tactical plan** is concerned with what the lower level units within each division must do, how they must do it, and who is in charge at each level. Tactics are the means needed to activate a strategy and make it work.

Tactical plans are concerned with shorter time frames and narrower scopes than are strategic plans. These plans usually span one year or less because they are considered short-term goals. Long-term goals, on the other hand, can take several years or more to accomplish. Normally, it is the middle manager's responsibility to take the broad strategic plan and identify specific tactical actions.

Strategic plans

A **strategic plan** is an outline of steps designed with the goals of the entire organization as a whole in mind, rather than with the goals of specific divisions or departments. Strategic planning begins with an organization's mission.

Strategic plans look ahead over the next two, three, five, or even more years to move the organization from where it currently is to where it wants to be. Requiring multilevel involvement, these plans demand harmony among all levels of management within the organization. Top-level management develops the directional objectives for the entire organization, while lower levels of management develop compatible objectives and plans to achieve them. Top management's strategic plan for the entire organization becomes the framework and sets dimensions for the lower level planning.

Contingency plans

Intelligent and successful management depends upon a constant pursuit of adaptation, flexibility, and mastery of changing conditions. Strong management requires a "keeping all options open" approach at all times — that's where contingency planning comes in.

Contingency planning involves identifying alternative courses of action that can be implemented if and when the original plan proves inadequate because of changing circumstances.

Keep in mind that events beyond a manager's control may cause even the most carefully prepared alternative future scenarios to go awry. Unexpected problems and events frequently occur. When they do, managers may need to change their plans. Anticipating change during the planning process is best in case things don't go as expected. Management can then develop alternatives to the existing plan and ready them for use when and if circumstances make these alternatives appropriate.

Identifying Barriers to Planning

Various barriers can inhibit successful planning. In order for plans to be effective and to yield the desired results, managers must identify any potential barriers and work to overcome them. The common barriers that inhibit successful planning are as follows:

- **Inability to plan or inadequate planning.** Managers are not born with the ability to plan. Some managers are not successful planners because they lack the background, education, and/or ability. Others may have never been taught how to plan. When these two types of managers take the time to plan, they may not know how to conduct planning as a process.

- **Lack of commitment to the planning process.** The development of of a plan is hard work; it is much easier for a manager to claim that he or she doesn't have the time to work through the required planning process than to actually devote the time to developing a plan. (The latter, of course, would save them more time in the long run!) Another possible reason for lack of commitment can be fear of failure. As a result, managers may choose to do little or nothing to help in the planning process.

- **Inferior information.** Facts that are out-of-date, of poor quality, or of insufficient quantity can be major barriers to planning. No matter how well managers plan, if they are basing their planning on inferior information, their plans will probably fail.

- **Focusing on the present at the expense of the future.** Failure to consider the long-term effects of a plan because of emphasis on short-term problems may lead to trouble in preparing for the future. Managers should try to keep the big picture — their long-term goals — in mind when developing their plans.

- **Too much reliance on the organization's planning department.** Many companies have a planning department or a planning and development team. These departments conduct studies, do research, build models, and project probable results, but they do not implement plans.

Planning department results are aids in planning and should be used only as such. Formulating the plan is still the manager's responsibility.

■ **Concentrating on controllable variables.** Managers can find themselves concentrating on the things and events that they can control, such as new product development, but then fail to consider outside factors, such as a poor economy. One reason may be that managers demonstrate a decided preference for the known and an aversion to the unknown.

The good news about these barriers is that they can all be overcome. To plan successfully, managers need to use effective communication, acquire quality information, and solicit the involvement of others.

Chapter Checkout

Q&A

1. The managerial function that provides direction, a common sense of purpose for the organization through the development of goals and objectives, and the means to reach them is _____.
   a. planning
   b. controlling
   c. leading
   d. organizing

2. The statement that explains the primary purpose of the organization and why the organization exists is the _____.
   a. budget
   b. strategic plan
   c. mission statement
   d. operational plan

3. Plans that usually span one year or less, are developed by middle managers, and are concerned with what the major subsystems within each organization must do are _____.
   a. strategic plans
   b. tactical plans
   c. operational plans
   d. contingency plans

4. Goals that are established by top management and relate to where the organization wants to be in the future are _____.
   a. operational objectives
   b. budgets
   c. standing goals
   d. strategic goals

5. All of the following are significant major barriers to effective planning except a(n) _____.
   a. lack of commitment to the planning process
   b. overreliance on the planning department
   c. overemphasis on the uncontrollable environmental factors
   d. lack of focus on the long term

Answers: 1. a **2.** c **3.** b **4.** d **5.** c

Chapter 6

CREATING ORGANIZATIONAL STRUCTURE

Chapter Check-In

❏ Figuring out how planning and organizing coincide

❏ Understanding the different forms of organizational structures

❏ Noting the differences between formal and informal organizational structures

The second function of management is organizing. After a manager has a plan in place, she can structure her teams and resources. This important step can profoundly affect an organization's success.

Not only does a business's organizational structure help determine how well its employees make decisions, but it also reflects how well they respond to problems. These responses, over time, can make or break an organization. In addition, the organizational structure influences employees' attitudes toward their work. A suitable organizational structure can minimize a business's costs, as well as maximize its efficiency, which increases its ability to compete in a global economy. For these reasons, many businesses have tinkered with their organizational structures in recent years in efforts to enhance their profits and competitive edge.

In this chapter, organizational structures are examined in detail. Topics include the development of organizational structures, including how tasks and responsibilities are organized through specialization and departmentalization. In addition, some of the forms organizational structures may take are also explored. Finally, the differences between formal and informal organizational structures are addressed.

The Relationship between Planning and Organizing

Once managers have their plans in place, they need to organize the necessary resources to accomplish their goals. **Organizing,** the second of the universal management functions, is the process of establishing the orderly use of resources by assigning and coordinating tasks. The organizing process transforms plans into reality through the purposeful deployment of people and resources within a decision-making framework known as the organizational structure.

The organizational structure is defined as

- The set of formal tasks assigned to individuals and departments

- The formal reporting relationships, including lines of authority, decision responsibility, number of hierarchical levels, and span of managerial control

- The design of systems to ensure effective coordination of employees across departments

The organizational structure provides a framework for the hierarchy, or *vertical structure,* of the organization. An **organizational chart** is the visual representation of this vertical structure.

The Organizational Process

Organizing, like planning, must be a carefully worked out and applied process. This process involves determining what work is needed to accomplish the goal, assigning those tasks to individuals, and arranging those individuals in a decision-making framework (organizational structure). The end result of the organizing process is an **organization** — a whole consisting of unified parts acting in harmony to execute tasks to achieve goals, both effectively and efficiently.

A properly implemented organizing process should result in a work environment where all team members are aware of their responsibilities. If the organizing process is not conducted well, the results may yield confusion, frustration, loss of efficiency, and limited effectiveness.

In general, the organizational process consists of five steps (a flowchart of these steps is shown in Figure 6-1):

Figure 6-1 The organizational process.

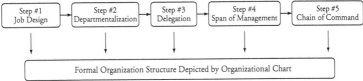

Step #1 Job Design → Step #2 Departmentalization → Step #3 Delegation → Step #4 Span of Management → Step #5 Chain of Command

Formal Organization Structure Depicted by Organizational Chart

1. **Review plans and objectives.**

   Objectives are the specific activities that must be completed to achieve goals. Plans shape the activities needed to reach those goals. Managers must examine plans initially and continue to do so as plans change and new goals are developed.

2. **Determine the work activities necessary to accomplish objectives.**

   Although this task may seem overwhelming to some managers, it doesn't need to be. Managers simply list and analyze all the tasks that need to be accomplished in order to reach organizational goals.

3. **Classify and group the necessary work activities into manageable units.**

   A manager can group activities based on four models of departmentalization: functional, geographical, product, and customer.

4. **Assign activities and delegate authority.**

   Managers assign the defined work activities to specific individuals. Also, they give each individual the authority (right) to carry out the assigned tasks. (For more on authority and delegation, see the respective sections later in this chapter.)

5. **Design a hierarchy of relationships.**

   A manager should determine the vertical (decision-making) and horizontal (coordinating) relationships of the organization as a whole. Next, using the organizational chart, a manager should diagram the relationships. (The horizontal organization is discussed in Chapter 7.)

Concepts of Organizing

The working relationships — vertical and horizontal associations between individuals and groups — that exist within an organization affect how its activities are accomplished and coordinated. Effective organizing depends on the mastery of several important concepts: work specialization, chain of command, authority, delegation, span of control, and centralization versus decentralization. Many of these concepts are based on the principles developed by Henri Fayol (see Chapter 2).

Work specialization

One popular organizational concept is based on the fundamental principle that employees can work more efficiently if they're allowed to specialize. **Work specialization,** sometimes called division of labor, is the degree to which organizational tasks are divided into separate jobs. Employees within each department perform only the tasks related to their specialized function.

When specialization is extensive, employees specialize in a single task, such as running a particular machine in a factory assembly line. Jobs tend to be small, but workers can perform them efficiently. By contrast, if a single factory employee built an entire automobile or performed a large number of unrelated jobs in a bottling plant, the results would be inefficient.

Despite the apparent advantages of specialization, many organizations are moving away from this principle. With too much specialization, employees are isolated and perform only small, narrow, boring tasks. In addition, if that person leaves the company, his specialized knowledge may disappear as well. Many companies are enlarging jobs to provide greater challenges and creating teams so that employees can rotate among several jobs.

Chain of command

The **chain of command** is an unbroken line of authority that links all persons in an organization and defines who reports to whom. This chain has two underlying principles: unity of command and scalar principle.

- **Unity of command:** This principle states that an employee should have one and only one supervisor to whom he or she is directly responsible. No employee should report to two or more people. Otherwise, the employee may receive conflicting demands or priorities from several supervisors at once, placing this employee in a no-win situation.

  Sometimes, however, an organization deliberately breaks the chain of command, such as when a project team is created to work on a special project. In such cases, team members report to their immediate supervisor and also to a team project leader. Another example is when a sales representative reports to both an immediate district supervisor and a marketing specialist, who is coordinating the introduction of a new product, in the home office.

Nevertheless, these examples are exceptions to the rule. They happen under special circumstances and usually only within a special type of employee group. For the most part, however, when allocating tasks to individuals or grouping assignments, management should ensure that each has one boss, and only one boss, to whom he or she directly reports.

■ **Scalar principle:** The scalar principle refers to a clearly defined line of authority that includes all employees in the organization. The classical school of management suggests that there should be a clear and unbroken chain of command linking every person in the organization with successively higher levels of authority up to and including the top manager. When organizations grow in size, they tend to get taller, as more and more levels of management are added. This increases overhead costs, adds more communication layers, and impacts understanding and access between top and bottom levels. It can greatly slow decision making and can lead to a loss of contact with the client or customer.

Authority

Authority is the formal and legitimate right of a manager to make decisions, issue orders, and allocate resources to achieve organizationally desired outcomes. A manager's authority is defined in his or her job description.

Organizational authority has three important underlying principles:

■ Authority is based on the organizational position, and anyone in the same position has the same authority.

■ Authority is accepted by subordinates. Subordinates comply because they believe that managers have a legitimate right to issue orders.

■ Authority flows down the vertical hierarchy. Positions at the top of the hierarchy are vested with more formal authority than are positions at the bottom.

In addition, authority comes in three types:

■ **Line authority** gives a manager the right to direct the work of his or her employees and make many decisions without consulting others. Line managers are always in charge of essential activities such as sales, and they are authorized to issue orders to subordinates down the chain of command.

- **Staff authority** supports line authority by advising, servicing, and assisting, but this type of authority is typically limited. For example, the assistant to the department head has staff authority because he or she acts as an extension of that authority. These assistants can give advice and suggestions, but they don't have to be obeyed. The department head may also give the assistant the authority to act, such as the right to sign off on expense reports or memos. In such cases, the directives are given under the line authority of the boss.

- **Functional authority** is authority delegated to an individual or department over specific activities undertaken by personnel in other departments. Staff managers may have functional authority, meaning that they can issue orders down the chain of command within the very narrow limits of their authority. For example, supervisors in a manufacturing plant may find that their immediate bosses have line authority over them, but that someone in corporate headquarters may also have line authority over some of their activities or decisions.

  Why would an organization create positions of functional authority? After all, this authority breaks the unity of command principle by having individuals report to two bosses. The answer is that functional authority allows specialization of skills and improved coordination. This concept was originally suggested by Frederick Taylor (see Chapter 2). He separated "planning" from "doing" by establishing a special department to relieve the laborer and the foreman from the work of planning. The role of the foreman became one of making sure that planned operations were carried out. The major problem of functional authority is overlapping relationships, which can be resolved by clearly designating to individuals which activities their immediate bosses have authority over and which activities are under the direction of someone else.

Delegation

A concept related to authority is **delegation.** Delegation is the downward transfer of authority from a manager to a subordinate. Most organizations today encourage managers to delegate authority in order to provide maximum flexibility in meeting customer needs. In addition, delegation leads to empowerment, in that people have the freedom to contribute ideas and do their jobs in the best possible ways. This involvement can increase job satisfaction for the individual and frequently results in better job performance. Without delegation, managers do all the work themselves and underutilize their workers. The ability to delegate is crucial to managerial success. Managers need to take four steps if they want to successfully delegate responsibilities to their teams.

1. **Specifically assign tasks to individual team members.**

   The manager needs to make sure that employees know that they are ultimately responsible for carrying out specific assignments.

2. **Give team members the correct amount of authority to accomplish assignments.**

   Typically, an employee is assigned authority commensurate with the task. A classical principle of organization warns managers not to delegate without giving the subordinate the authority to perform to delegated task. When an employee has responsibility for the task outcome but little authority, accomplishing the job is possible but difficult. The subordinate without authority must rely on persuasion and luck to meet performance expectations. When an employee has authority exceeding responsibility, he or she may become a tyrant, using authority toward frivolous outcomes.

3. **Make sure that team members accept responsibility.**

   Responsibility is the flip side of the authority coin. Responsibility is the duty to perform the task or activity an employee has been assigned. An important distinction between authority and responsibility is that the supervisor delegates authority, but the responsibility is shared. Delegation of authority gives a subordinate the right to make commitments, use resources, and take actions in relation to duties assigned. However, in making this delegation, the obligation created is not shifted from the supervisor to the subordinate — it is shared. A supervisor always retains some responsibility for work performed by lower-level units or individuals.

4. **Create accountability.**

   Team members need to know that they are accountable for their projects. **Accountability** means answering for one's actions and accepting the consequences. Team members may need to report and justify task outcomes to their superiors. Managers can build accountability into their organizational structures by monitoring performances and rewarding successful outcomes. Although managers are encouraged to delegate authority, they often find accomplishing this step difficult for the following reasons:

- Delegation requires planning, and planning takes time. A manager may say, "By the time I explain this task to someone, I could do it myself." This manager is overlooking the fact that the initial time spent up front training someone to do a task may save much more time in the long run. Once an employee has learned how to do a task, the manager will not have to take the time to show that employee how to do it again. This improves the flow of the process from that point forward.

- Managers may simply lack confidence in the abilities of their subordinates. Such a situation fosters the attitude, "If you want it done well, do it yourself." If managers feel that their subordinates lack abilities, they need to provide appropriate training so that all are comfortable performing their duties.

- Managers experience dual accountability. Managers are accountable for their own actions and the actions of their subordinates. If a subordinate fails to perform a certain task or does so poorly, the manager is ultimately responsible for the subordinate's failure. But by the same token, if a subordinate succeeds, the manager shares in that success as well, and the department can be even more productive.

- Finally, managers may refrain from delegating because they are insecure about their value to the organization. However, managers need to realize that they become more valuable as their teams become more productive and talented.

Despite the perceived disadvantages of delegation, the reality is that a manager can improve the performance of his or her work groups by empowering subordinates through effective delegation. Few managers are successful in the long term without learning to delegate effectively.

So, how do managers learn to delegate effectively? The following additional principles may be helpful for managers who've tried to delegate in the past and failed:

- **Principle 1: Match the employee to the task.** Managers should carefully consider the employees to whom they delegate tasks. The individual selected should possess the skills and capabilities needed to complete the task. Perhaps even more important is to delegate to an individual who is not only able to complete the task but also willing to complete the task. Therefore, managers should delegate to employees who will view their accomplishments as personal benefits.

■ **Principle 2: Be organized and communicate clearly.** The manager must have a clear understanding of what needs to be done, what deadlines exist, and what special skills are required. Furthermore, managers must be capable of communicating their instructions effectively if their subordinates are to perform up to their expectations.

■ **Principle 3: Transfer authority and accountability with the task.** The delegation process is doomed to failure if the individual to whom the task is delegated is not given the authority to succeed at accomplishing the task and is not held accountable for the results as well. Managers must expect employees to carry the ball and then let them do so. This means providing the employees with the necessary resources and power to succeed, giving them timely feedback on their progress, and holding them fully accountable for the results of their efforts. Managers also should be available to answer questions as needed.

■ **Principle 4: Choose the level of delegation carefully.** Delegation does not mean that the manager can walk away from the task or the person to whom the task is delegated. The manager must maintain some control of both the process and the results of the delegated activities. Depending upon the confidence the manager has in the subordinate and the importance of the task, the manager can choose to delegate at several levels.

Span of control

Span of control (sometimes called span of management) refers to the number of workers who report to one manager. For hundreds of years, theorists have searched for an ideal span of control. When no perfect number of subordinates for a manager to supervise became apparent, they turned their attention to the more general issue of whether the span should be wide or narrow.

A wide span of management exists when a manager has a large number of subordinates. Generally, the span of control may be wide when

■ The manager and the subordinates are very competent.

■ The organization has a well-established set of standard operating procedures.

■ Few new problems are anticipated.

A narrow span of management exists when the manager has only a few subordinates. The span should be narrow when

- Workers are located far from one another physically.

- The manager has a lot of work to do in addition to supervising workers.

- A great deal of interaction is required between supervisor and workers.

- New problems arise frequently.

Keep in mind that the span of management may change from one department to another within the same organization.

Centralization versus decentralization

The general pattern of authority throughout an organization determines the extent to which that organization is centralized or decentralized.

A **centralized organization** systematically works to concentrate authority at the upper levels. In a **decentralized organization,** management consciously attempts to spread authority to the lower organization levels.

A variety of factors can influence the extent to which a firm is centralized or decentralized. The following is a list of possible determinants:

- **The external environment in which the firm operates.** The more complex and unpredictable this environment, the more likely it is that top management will let low-level managers make important decisions. After all, low-level managers are closer to the problems because they are more likely to have direct contact with customers and workers. Therefore, they are in a better position to determine problems and concerns.

- **The nature of the decision itself.** The riskier or the more important the decision, the greater the tendency to centralize decision making.

- **The abilities of low-level managers.** If these managers do not have strong decision-making skills, top managers will be reluctant to decentralize. Strong low-level decision-making skills encourage decentralization.

- **The organization's tradition of management.** An organization that has traditionally practiced centralization or decentralization is likely to maintain that posture in the future.

In principle, neither philosophy is right or wrong. What works for one organization may or may not work for another. Kmart Corporation and McDonald's have both been very successful — both practice centralization. By the same token, decentralization has worked very well for General Electric and Sears. Every organization must assess its own situation and then choose the level of centralization or decentralization that works best.

The Informal Organization

In addition to the formal organizational structures covered throughout this chapter, an organization may also have a hidden side that doesn't show up on its organizational chart. This hidden *informal organization* is defined by the patterns, behaviors, and interactions that stem from personal rather than official relationships.

In the informal organization, the emphasis is on people and their relationships; in the formal organization, the emphasis is on official organizational positions. The leverage, or clout, in the informal organization is informal power that's attached to a specific individual. On the other hand, in the formal organization, formal authority comes directly from the position. An individual retains formal authority only so long as he or she occupies the position. Informal power is personal; authority is organizational.

Firmly embedded within every informal organization are informal groups and the notorious grapevine; the following list offers descriptions of each:

- **Informal groups.** Workers may create an informal group to go bowling, form a union, discuss work challenges, or have lunch together every day. The group may last for several years or only a few hours.

  Sometimes employees join these informal groups simply because of its goals. Other times, they simply want to be with others who are similar to them. Still others may join informal groups simply because they want to be accepted by their coworkers.

- **The grapevine.** The grapevine is the informal communications network within an organization. It is completely separate from — and sometimes much faster than — the organization's formal channels of communication.

  Formal communication usually follows a path that parallels the organizational chain of command. By contrast, information can be transmitted through the grapevine in any direction — up, down, diagonally, or horizontally across the organizational structure. Subordinates may pass information to their bosses, an executive may relay something to a maintenance worker, or employees in different departments may share tidbits. Communication is discussed in Chapter 13.

Grapevine information may be concerned with topics ranging from the latest management decisions to the results of today's World Series game to pure gossip. The information may be important or of little interest. By the same token, the information on the grapevine may be highly accurate or totally distorted.

The informal organization of a firm may be more important than a manager realizes. Although managers may think that the informal organization is nothing more than rumors that are spread among the employees, it is actually a very important tool in maintaining company-wide information flow. Results of studies show that the office grapevine is 75 percent to 90 percent accurate and provides managers and staff with better information than formal communications.

Rather than ignore or try to suppress the grapevine, managers should make an attempt to tune in to it. In fact, they should identify the people in the organization who are key to the information flow and feed them information that they can spread to others. Managers should make as big an effort to know who their internal disseminators of information are as they do to find the proper person to send a press release. Managers can make good use of the power of the informal organization and the grapevine.

Chapter Checkout

Q&A

1. The unbroken line of relationships from the bottom to the top of an organization is called the _____.
   a. span of control
   b. unity of command
   c. division of labor
   d. chain of command

2. The degree to which organizational tasks are subdivided into separate work jobs is called _____.
   a. decentralization
   b. division of labor
   c. span of control
   d. centralization

3. The formal and legitimate right of a manager to make decisions, give orders, and allocate resources is known as _____.

   a. accountability

   b. power

   c. authority

   d. responsibility

4. The philosophy of management that focuses upon systematically retaining authority at the top of the organization is called _____.

   a. centralization

   b. decentralization

   c. departmentalization

   d. specialization

5. Which of the following statements does not correctly characterize the difference between the formal and the informal organization?

   a. In the formal organization, the formal organization authority comes from the position.

   b. Informal power follows the chain of command, but authority does not.

   c. Leverage in the informal organization is informal power that goes with the person.

   d. Groups give power in the informal organization.

Answers: 1. d **2.** b **3.** c **4.** a **5.** b

Chapter 7

ORGANIZATIONAL DESIGN
AND STRUCTURE

Chapter Check-In

❏ Defining organizational design

❏ Differentiating between mechanistic and organic structures

❏ Identifying the factors that affect organizational design

❏ Recognizing different organizational structures

Few things endure long term without being changed. Even well-known brand names, familiar slogans, and classic songs face updates in today's changing culture. Organizations are no different, and must respond to changes in their environments as well. Whether it's technology upgrades to meet customer demands or policy updates to accommodate employee growth, managers must be both willing and able to deal with the challenges of change.

In this chapter, the elements of organizational design are discussed. In addition, the importance of a manager's ability to adapt his or her organizational structure to fit the changing times is examined. The basic organizational structures and the importance of recognizing the factors that affect the design of these structures are also studied.

Organizational Design Defined

An organization's structure is defined by its configuration and interrelationships of positions and departments. **Organizational design** is the creation or change of an organization's structure. The organizational design of a company reflects its efforts to respond to changes, integrate new elements, ensure collaboration, and allow flexibility.

Organizing a business is difficult. Once an organization has a plan (see Chapter 5), the next step is to make it happen. Discussing the major characteristics of organizational structure (see Chapter 6) is, in many ways, like discussing the important parts of a jigsaw puzzle one by one. This chapter assembles those puzzle pieces. In particular, the two basic forms of organizational structure—mechanistic and organic—will be discussed.

Bureaucracy Basics

In the past, organizations were commonly structured as bureaucracies. A *bureaucracy* is a form of organization based on logic, order, and the legitimate use of formal authority. Bureaucracies are meant to be orderly, fair, and highly efficient. Their features include a clear-cut division of labor, strict hierarchy of authority, formal rules and procedures, and promotion based on competency.

Today, many people view bureaucracies negatively and recognize that bureaucracies have their limits. If organizations rely too much on rules and procedures, they become unwieldy and too rigid—making them slow to respond to changing environments and more likely to perish in the long run.

But management theory doesn't view all bureaucratic structures as inevitably flawed. Instead, they ask these critical questions:

- When is a bureaucracy a good choice for an organization?

- What alternatives exist when a bureaucracy is not a good choice?

Research, conducted in England by Tom Burns and George Stalker in the early 1960s, attempted to answer these questions. Burns and Stalker studied industrial firms to determine how the nature of each firm's environment affected the way the firm was organized and managed. They believed a stable, unchanging environment demanded a different type of organization than a rapidly changing one. Although a stable environment worked well under a bureaucracy, managers in constantly changing, innovative environments needed an organizational structure that allowed them to be responsive and creative.

As a result, two distinct frameworks, the mechanistic and organic structures, were identified.

The mechanistic structure

The **mechanistic structure**, sometimes used synonymously with bureaucratic structure, is a management system based on a formal framework of authority that is carefully outlined and precisely followed. An organization that uses a mechanistic structure is likely to have the following characteristics:

- Clearly specified tasks

- Precise definitions of the rights and obligations of members

- Clearly defined line and staff positions with formal relationships between the two

- Tendency toward formal communication throughout the organizational structure

Perhaps the best example of a mechanistic structure is found in a college or university. Consider the very rigid and formal college entrance and registration procedures. The reason for such procedures is to ensure that the organization is able to deal with a large number of people in an equitable and fair manner. Although many individuals do not like them, regulations and standard operating procedures pretty much guarantee uniform treatment. But those same rules and procedures, with their time-consuming communication and decision-making processes, tend to bog down organizations.

Mechanistic organizations are appropriate when the external environment is fairly stable. The biggest drawback to the mechanistic structure is its lack of flexibility, which may cause an organization to have trouble adjusting to change and coping with the unexpected.

The organic structure

The organic structure tends to work better in dynamic environments where managers need to react quickly to change. An **organic structure** is a management system founded on cooperation and knowledge-based authority. It is much less formal than a mechanistic organization, and much more flexible. Organic structures are characterized by

- Roles that are not highly defined.

- Tasks that are continually redefined.

- Little reliance on formal authority.

- Decentralized control.

- Fast decision making.

- Informal patterns of both delegation and communication.

Because the atmosphere is informal and the lines of authority may shift depending on the situation, the organic structure requires more cooperation among employees than does a bureaucracy.

One example of an organic structure is the Salvation Army. Although branches are located throughout the nation, the organization does not have a complex structure; it encourages different units to take on new challenges. The Salvation Army does not rely heavily on written rules and procedures. Therefore, this organization can create the procedures that work best as different situations arise. The Salvation Army's ability to take on new tasks and to fulfill its mission regardless of the circumstances it faces is one reason why it's a hallmark of organic organizations.

Factors Affecting Organizational Design

Although many things can affect the choice of an appropriate structure for an organization, the following five factors are the most common: size, life cycle, strategy, environment, and technology. The following sections examine these roles in organizational design.

Organizational size

The larger an organization becomes, the more complicated its structure. When an organization is small — such as a single retail store, a two-person consulting firm, or a restaurant — its structure can be simple.

In reality, if the organization is very small, it may not even have a formal structure. Instead of following an organizational chart or specified job functions, individuals simply perform tasks based on their likes, dislikes, ability, and/or need. Rules and guidelines are not prevalent and may exist only to provide the parameters within which organizational members can make decisions. Small organizations are very often organic systems.

As an organization grows, however, it becomes increasingly difficult to manage without more formal work assignments and some delegation of authority. Therefore, large organizations develop formal structures. Tasks are highly specialized, and detailed rules and guidelines dictate work procedures. Interorganizational communication flows primarily from superior to subordinate, and hierarchical relationships serve as the foundation for authority, responsibility, and control. The type of structure that develops will be one that provides the organization with the ability to operate effectively. That's one reason larger organizations are often mechanistic— mechanistic systems are usually designed to maximize specialization and improve efficiency.

Organization life cycle

Organizations, like humans, tend to progress through stages known as a life cycle. Like humans, most organizations go through the following four stages: birth, youth, midlife, and maturity. Each stage has characteristics that have implications for the structure of the firm.

- **Birth:** In the birth state, a firm is just beginning. An organization in the birth stage does not yet have a formal structure. In a young organization, there is not much delegation of authority. The founder usually "calls the shots."

- **Youth:** In this phase, the organization is trying to grow. The emphasis in this stage is on becoming larger. The company shifts its attention from the wishes of the founder to the wishes of the customer. The organization becomes more organic in structure during this phase. It is during this phase that the formal structure is designed, and some delegation of authority occurs.

- **Midlife:** This phase occurs when the organization has achieved a high level of success. An organization in midlife is larger, with a more complex and increasingly formal structure. More levels appear in the chain of command, and the founder may have difficulty remaining in control. As the organization becomes older, it may also become more mechanistic in structure.

- **Maturity:** Once a firm has reached the maturity phase, it tends to become less innovative, less interested in expanding, and more interested in maintaining itself in a stable, secure environment. The emphasis is on improving efficiency and profitability. However, in an attempt to improve efficiency and profitability, the firm often tends to become less innovative. Stale products result in sales declines and reduced profitability. Organizations in this stage are slowly dying. However, maturity is not an inevitable stage. Firms experiencing the decline of maturity may institute the changes necessary to revitalize. (Chapter 8 discusses how to manage change.)

Although an organization may proceed sequentially through all four stages, it does not have to. An organization may skip a phase, or it may cycle back to an earlier phase. An organization may even try to change its position in the life cycle by changing its structure.

As the life-cycle concept implies, a relationship exists between an organization's size and age. As organizations age, they tend to get larger; thus, the structural changes a firm experiences as it gets larger and the changes it experiences as it progresses through the life cycle are parallel. Therefore, the older the organization and the larger the organization, the greater its need for more structure, more specialization of tasks, and more rules. As a result, the older and larger the organization becomes, the greater the likelihood that it will move from an organic structure to a mechanistic structure.

Strategy

How an organization is going to position itself in the market in terms of its product is considered its strategy. A company may decide to be always the first on the market with the newest and best product (differentiation strategy), or it may decide that it will produce a product already on the market more efficiently and more cost effectively (cost-leadership strategy). Each of these strategies requires a structure that helps the organization reach its objectives. In other words, the structure must fit the strategy.

Companies that want to be the first on the market with the newest and best product probably are organic, because organic structures permit organizations to respond quickly to changes. Companies that elect to produce the same products more efficiently and effectively will probably be mechanistic.

Environment

The environment is the world in which the organization operates, and includes conditions that influence the organization such as economic, social-cultural, legal-political, technological, and natural environment conditions. Environments are often described as either stable or dynamic.

- In a **stable environment,** the customers' desires are well understood and probably will remain consistent for a relatively long time. Examples of organizations that face relatively stable environments include manufacturers of staple items such as detergent, cleaning supplies, and paper products.

- In a **dynamic environment,** the customers' desires are continuously changing—the opposite of a stable environment. This condition is often thought of as turbulent. In addition, the technology that a company uses while in this environment may need to be continuously improved and updated. An example of an industry functioning in a dynamic environment is electronics. Technology changes create competitive pressures for all electronics industries, because as technology changes, so do the desires of consumers.

In general, organizations that operate in stable external environments find mechanistic structures to be advantageous. This system provides a level of efficiency that enhances the long-term performances of organizations that enjoy relatively stable operating environments. In contrast, organizations that operate in volatile and frequently changing environments are more likely to find that an organic structure provides the greatest benefits. This structure allows the organization to respond to environment change more proactively.

Technology

Advances in technology are the most frequent cause of change in organizations since they generally result in greater efficiency and lower costs for the firm. Technology is the way tasks are accomplished using tools, equipment, techniques, and human know-how.

In the early 1960s, Joan Woodward found that the right combination of structure and technology were critical to organizational success. She conducted a study of technology and structure in more than 100 English manufacturing firms, which she classified into three categories of core-manufacturing technology:

- **Small-batch production** is used to manufacture a variety of custom, made-to-order goods. Each item is made somewhat differently to meet a customer's specifications. A print shop is an example of a business that uses small-batch production.

- **Mass production** is used to create a large number of uniform goods in an assembly-line system. Workers are highly dependent on one another, as the product passes from stage to stage until completion. Equipment may be sophisticated, and workers often follow detailed instructions while performing simplified jobs. A company that bottles soda pop is an example of an organization that utilizes mass production.

- Organizations using **continuous-process production** create goods by continuously feeding raw materials, such as liquid, solids, and gases, through a highly automated system. Such systems are equipment intensive, but can often be operated by a relatively small labor force. Classic examples are automated chemical plants and oil refineries.

Woodward discovered that small-batch and continuous processes had more flexible structures, and the best mass-production operations were more rigid structures.

Once again, organizational design depends on the type of business. The small-batch and continuous processes work well in organic structures and mass production operations work best in mechanistic structures.

Five Approaches to Organizational Design

Managers must make choices about how to group people together to perform their work. Five common approaches — functional, divisional, matrix, team, and networking—help managers determine departmental groupings (grouping of positions into departments). The five structures are basic organizational structures, which are then adapted to an organization's needs. All five approaches, outlined in the following sections, combine varying elements of mechanistic and organic structures. For example, the organizational design trend today incorporates a minimum of bureaucratic features and displays more features of the organic design with a decentralized authority structure, fewer rules and procedures, and so on.

Functional structure

The **functional structure** groups positions into work units based on similar activities, skills, expertise, and resources (see Figure 7-1 for a functional organizational chart). Production, marketing, finance, and human resources are common groupings within a functional structure.

Figure 7-1 The functional structure.

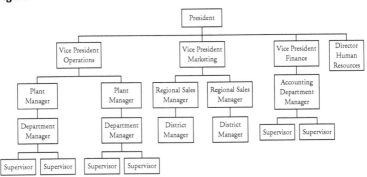

As the simplest approach, a functional structure features well-defined channels of communication and authority/responsibility relationships (see

Chapter 6). Not only can this structure improve productivity by minimizing duplication of personnel and equipment, but it also makes employees comfortable and simplifies training as well.

But the functional structure has many downsides that may make it inappropriate for some organizations. Here are a few examples:

■ The functional structure can result in narrowed perspectives because of the separateness of different department work groups. Managers may have a hard time relating to marketing, for example, which is often in an entirely different grouping. As a result, anticipating or reacting to changing consumer needs may be difficult. In addition, reduced cooperation and communication may occur.

■ Decisions and communication are slow to take place because of the many layers of hierarchy. Authority is more centralized.

■ The functional structure gives managers experience in only one field—their own. Managers do not have the opportunity to see how all the firm's departments work together and understand their interrelationships and interdependence. In the long run, this specialization results in executives with narrow backgrounds and little training handling top management duties.

Divisional structure

Because managers in large companies may have difficulty keeping track of all their company's products and activities, specialized departments may develop. These departments are divided according to their organizational outputs. Examples include departments created to distinguish among production, customer service, and geographical categories. This grouping of departments is called divisional structure (see Figure 7-2). These departments allow managers to better focus their resources and results. Divisional structure also makes performance easier to monitor. As a result, this structure is flexible and responsive to change.

However, divisional structure does have its drawbacks. Because managers are so specialized, they may waste time duplicating each other's activities and resources. In addition, competition among divisions may develop due to limited resources.

Figure 7-2 The divisional structure—Disney in the early 1990s.

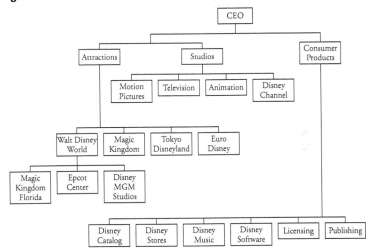

Matrix structure

The matrix structure combines functional specialization with the focus of divisional structure (see Figure 7-3). This structure uses permanent cross-functional teams to integrate functional expertise with a divisional focus.

Employees in a matrix structure belong to at least two formal groups at the same time—a functional group and a product, program, or project team. They also report to two bosses—one within the functional group and the other within the team.

This structure not only increases employee motivation, but it also allows technical and general management training across functional areas as well. Potential advantages include

■ Better cooperation and problem solving.

■ Increased flexibility.

■ Better customer service.

■ Better performance accountability.

■ Improved strategic management.

Figure 7-3 The matrix structure.

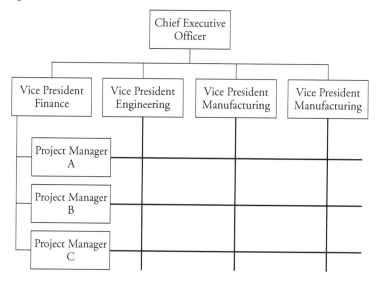

Predictably, the matrix structure also has potential disadvantages. Here are a few of this structure's drawbacks:

■ The two-boss system is susceptible to power struggles, as functional supervisors and team leaders vie with one another to exercise authority.

■ Members of the matrix may suffer task confusion when taking orders from more than one boss.

■ Teams may develop strong team loyalties that cause a loss of focus on larger organization goals.

■ Adding the team leaders, a crucial component, to a matrix structure can result in increased costs.

Team structure

Team structure organizes separate functions into a group based on one overall objective (see Figure 7-4). These **cross-functional teams** are composed of members from different departments who work together as needed to solve problems and explore opportunities. The intent is to break down functional barriers among departments and create a more effective relationship for solving ongoing problems.

Figure 7-4 The team structure.

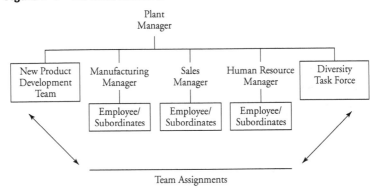

The team structure has many potential advantages, including the following:

- Intradepartmental barriers break down.

- Decision-making and response times speed up.

- Employees are motivated.

- Levels of managers are eliminated.

- Administrative costs are lowered.

The disadvantages include:

- Conflicting loyalties among team members.

- Time-management issues.

- Increased time spent in meetings.

Managers must be aware that how well team members work together often depends on the quality of interpersonal relations, group dynamics, and their team management abilities.

Network structure

The network structure relies on other organizations to perform critical functions on a contractual basis (see Figure 7-5). In other words, managers can contract out specific work to specialists.

Figure 7-5 The network structure.

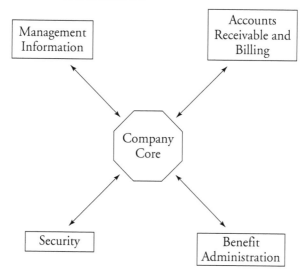

This approach provides flexibility and reduces overhead because the size of staff and operations can be reduced. On the other hand, the network structure may result in unpredictability of supply and lack of control because managers are relying on contractual workers to perform important work.

Chapter Checkout

Q&A

1. Which of the following would characterize a mechanistic structure?
   a. Free flow of information
   b. Few rules and regulations
   c. Centralized decision making
   d. All of the above

2. Which of the following organizations would most likely have an organic structure?

   a. A small organization utilizing small-batch technology in a changing environment

   b. A young organization operating in a very stable environment

   c. A large, old organization operating in a stable environment

   d. An old organization operating with mass production

3. Which of the following is not one of the advantages of the functional structure?

   a. Minimized duplication

   b. Quick response time to changes in the environment

   c. Well-defined channels of communication

   d. Simplified training

4. Which of the following statements characterizes the matrix structure?

   a. Communicating and coordination are decreased in the matrix structure.

   b. The matrix structure is the best of all possible structures and has few disadvantages.

   c. Although it's flexible, the matrix structures will always adversely affect the motivation level of the individual employee.

   d. The matrix structure is flexible and combines the advantages of functional specialization and the accountability of the divisional structure.

5. Which of the following is an important disadvantage of the team structure?

   a. Large amounts of time are required for employee meetings and training.

   b. It eliminates levels of management.

   c. It hurts employee motivation.

   d. Time required for decision making is increased.

Answers: 1. c **2.** a **3.** b **4.** d **5.** a.

Chapter 8

MANAGING CHANGE

Chapter Check-In

❑ Understanding factors that affect organizational changes

❑ Reviewing types of organizational changes

❑ Discerning how managers oversee planned changes

❑ Examining steps managers may take to implement changes

This is a time of unprecedented change in our society. The changes one experiences are happening at faster and faster rates. As examples, the telephone, radio, TV, and microwave weren't even in use decades ago, and today these gadgets are commonplace, along with the computer, Internet, and fax machine.

In just a few months, the technology that an organization uses on an everyday basis may be outdated and replaced. That means an organization needs to be responsive to advances in the technological environment; its employees' work skills must evolve as technology evolves. Organizations that refuse to adapt are likely to be the ones that won't be around in a few short years. If an organization wants to survive and prosper, its managers must continually innovate and adapt to new situations.

This chapter addresses the importance of managers stimulating and leading change in order to create organizations that have the ability to set aside old ways of thinking, the desire to become self-aware and open, the opportunity to learn how the whole organization works, and the commitment to develop a plan of action and work as a unit to accomplish the plan.

Causes of Organizational Change

Every organization goes through periods of transformation that can cause stress and uncertainty. To be successful, organizations must embrace many types of change. Businesses must develop improved production technologies, create new products desired in the marketplace, implement new administrative systems, and upgrade employees' skills. Organizations that adapt successfully are both profitable and admired.

Managers must contend with all factors that affect their organizations. The following lists internal and external environmental factors that can encourage organizational changes:

■ The **external environment** is affected by political, social, technological, and economic stimuli outside of the organization that cause changes.

■ The **internal environment** is affected by the organization's management policies and styles, systems, and procedures, as well as employee attitudes.

Typically, the concept of organizational change is used to describe organization-wide change, as opposed to smaller changes such as adding a new person, modifying a program, and so on. Examples of organization-wide change might include a change in mission, restructuring operations (for example, restructuring to self-managed teams or due to layoffs), new technologies, mergers, or new programs such as Total Quality Management, re-engineering, and so on.

Managers should note that all changes should be implemented as part of a strategy to accomplish an overall goal; these transformations should not take place just for the sake of change.

Types of Organizational Change

For organizations, the last decade has been fraught with restructurings, process enhancements, mergers, acquisitions, and layoffs—all in hopes of achieving revenue growth and increased profitability.

While the external environment (competitive, regulatory, and so on) will continue to play a role in an organization's ability to deliver goods and services, the internal environment within the organization will increasingly inhibit it from delivering products required to meet the demands of the marketplace unless it is able to adapt quickly. The major areas of changes in a company's internal environment include:

■ **Strategic:** Sometimes in the course of normal business operation it is necessary for management to adjust the firm's strategy to achieve the goals of the company, or even to change the mission statement of the organization in response to demands of the external environments. Adjusting a company's strategy may involve changing its fundamental approach to doing business: the markets it will target, the kinds of products it will sell, how they will be sold, its overall strategic orientation, the level of global activity, and its various partnerships and other joint-business arrangements.

■ **Structural:** Organizations often find it necessary to redesign the structure of the company due to influences from the external environment. Structural changes involve the hierarchy of authority, goals, structural characteristics, administrative procedures, and management systems. Almost all change in how an organization is managed falls under the category of structural change. A structural change may be as simple as implementing a no-smoking policy, or as involved as restructuring the company to meet the customer needs more effectively.

■ **Process-oriented:** Organizations may need to reengineer processes to achieve optimum workflow and productivity. Process-oriented change is often related to an organization's production process or how the organization assembles products or delivers services. The adoption of robotics in a manufacturing plant or of laser-scanning checkout systems at supermarkets are examples of process-oriented changes.

■ **People-centered:** This type of change alters the attitudes, behaviors, skills, or performance of employees in the company. Changing people-centered processes involves communicating, motivating, leading, and interacting within groups. This focus may entail changing how problems are solved, the way employees learn new skills, and even the very nature of how employees perceive themselves, their jobs and the organization.

Some people-centered changes may involve only incremental changes or small improvements in a process. For example, many organizations undergo leadership training that teaches managers how to communicate more openly with employees. Other programs may concentrate on team processes by teaching both managers and employees to work together more effectively to solve problems.

Remember that strategic, structural, process-oriented, and people-centered changes occur continuously in dynamic businesses. Often, changes in one of these areas impact changes in the other areas.

Many employees believe that a change is often reactive and nothing more than a quick fix; then they brace themselves for more changes in the future.

Management needs to realize that serious underlying problems in organizations must be addressed with long-term consequences in mind. Thus, when management implements changes, careful thought must be given to ensure that the new processes are for the long-term good of the company.

Challenges of Organizational Change

Planning and managing change, both cultural and technological, is one of the most challenging elements of a manager's job.

Obviously, the more a manager can plan in anticipation of a change, the better she serves her subordinates and the organization. Diagnosing the causes of change and structuring a program to promote a smooth transition to the new process, structure, and so on, is critical to a manager's success.

Managers need to be aware that organizations change in a number of dimensions that often relate to one another. These dimensions include

- **Extent of planning:** Although experts differ about how much change can be planned, managers still need to take steps to set up conditions that permit and even encourage change to occur.

- **Degree of change:** Changes may be incremental (relatively small, involving fine-tuning processes and behaviors within just one system or level of the organization) or quantum (significant change altering how a company operates).

- **Degree of learning:** This dimension relates to the degree to which organizational members are actively involved in learning how to plan and implement change while helping solve an existing problem (see Chapter 12).

- **Target of change:** Organizational change programs can vary with respect to the hierarchical level or functional area of which the change is targeted. Some changes are designed to influence top management and assist them in becoming stronger leaders. Other change programs may involve basic learning, such as customer services techniques for lower level employees.

- **Organization's structure:** Is it very stiff and bureaucratic? Is there a need for emphasis on policies, procedures, and rules? Some organizations are very stiff and bureaucratic and may need to "loosen up." Other organizations may suffer from lack of organization structure. They may need to emphasize policies, procedures, and rules.

Diagnosing the Need for Change

To plan change, managers must predict and diagnose the need for change. An organizational development theory developed by Larry E. Greiner is helpful in change management. Greiner's model shows an organization as it evolves through the five stages of growth, and the end of each of these stages is marked by a crisis that calls for a change. The five stages of growth are as follows:

1. **Creativity.** The founders of the organization dominate this stage, and the emphasis is on creating both a product and a market. But as the organization grows, management problems occur that cannot be handled through informal communication. The founders find themselves burdened with unwanted management responsibilities, and conflicts between the employees and management grow. It is at this point that the crisis of leadership occurs, and the first revolutionary period begins.

2. **Direction.** During this period, a strong manager, who is acceptable to the founder and who can pull the organization together, is appointed. During this phase the new manager and key staff take most of the responsibility for instituting direction, while lower level supervisors are treated more as functional specialists than autonomous decision-making managers. Lower level managers begin to demand more autonomy, and the next revolutionary period begins.

3. **Delegation.** This stage often poses problems for top managers who have been successful at being directive: They may find giving up responsibility difficult. Moreover, lower level managers generally are not accustomed to making decisions for themselves. As a result, numerous organizations flounder during this revolutionary period, adhering to centralized methods, while lower level employees grow disenchanted and leave the organization.

   When an organization gets to the growth stage of delegation, it usually begins to develop a decentralized organization structure, which heightens motivation at the lower levels. Eventually, the next crisis begins to evolve as the top managers sense that they are losing control over a highly diversified operation. The crisis of control results in a return to centralization, which is now inappropriate and creates resentment and hostility among those who had been given freedom.

4. **Control.** This stage is characterized by the use of formal systems for achieving greater coordination, with top management as the

watchdog. It results in the next revolutionary period, the crisis of red tape. This crisis most often occurs when the organization has become too large and complex, and is managed through formal programs and rigid systems. If the crisis of red tape is to be overcome, the organization must move to the next evolutionary phase.

5. **Collaboration.** The last of Greiner's phases emphasizes greater spontaneity in management action through teams and the skillful confrontation of interpersonal differences. Social control and self-discipline take over from formal action. Greiner's model shows uncertainty about what the next revolution of change will be, but anticipates that it will center on the psychological saturation of employees who grow emotionally and physically exhausted by the intensity of teamwork and the heavy pressure for innovative solutions.

To plan change, managers must predict and diagnose the need for change. Greiner's model of organizational growth and change can help managers understand how the need for change relates to the organizational cycles.

Steps in Planned Change

Once managers and an organization commit to planned change, they need to create a logical step-by step approach in order to accomplish the objectives. Planned change requires managers to follow an eight-step process for successful implementations, which is illustrated in Figure 8-1.

1. **Recognize the need for change.** Recognition of the need for change may occur at the top management level or in peripheral parts of the organization. The change may be due to either internal or external forces.

2. **Develop the goals of the change.** Remember that before any action is taken, it is necessary to determine why the change is necessary. Both problems and opportunities must be evaluated. Then it is important to define the needed changes in terms of products, technology, structure, and culture.

3. **Select a change agent.** The change agent is the person who takes leadership responsibility to implement planned change. The change agent must be alert to things that need revamping, open to good ideas, and supportive of the implementation of those ideas into actual practice.

Figure 8-1 Stages of planned change.

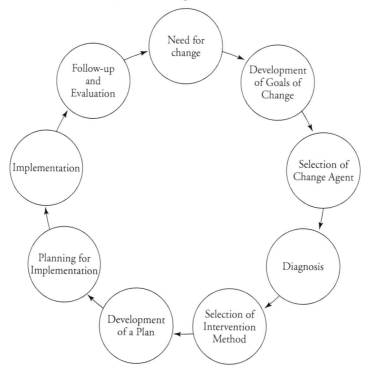

4. **Diagnose the current climate.** In this step, the change agent sets about gathering data about the climate of the organization in order to help employees prepare for change. Preparing people for change requires direct and forceful feedback about the negatives of the present situation, as compared to the desired future state, and sensitizing people to the forces of change that exist in their environment.

5. **Select an implementation method.** This step requires a decision on the best way to bring about the change. Managers can make themselves more sensitive to pressures for change by using networks of people and organizations with different perspectives and views, visiting other organizations exposed to new ideas, and using external standards of performance, such as competitor's progress.

6. **Develop a plan.** This step involves actually putting together the plan, or the "what" information. This phase also determines the when, where, and how of the plan. The plan is like a road map. It notes specific events and activities that must be timed and integrated to produce the change. It also delegates responsibility for each of the goals and objectives.

7. **Implement the plan.** After all the questions have been answered, the plan is put into operation. Once a change has begun, initial excitement can dissipate in the face of everyday problems. Managers can maintain the momentum for change by providing resources, developing new competencies and skills, reinforcing new behaviors, and building a support system for those initiating the change.

8. **Follow the plan and evaluate it.** During this step, managers must compare the actual results to the goals established in Step 4. It is important to determine whether the goals were met, and a complete follow-up and evaluation of the results aids this determination (Chapter 14 discusses evaluation). Change should produce positive results and not be undertaken for its own sake.

Keep in mind that a comprehensive model of planned change includes a set of activities that managers must engage in to manage the change process effectively. They must recognize the need for change, motivate change, create a vision, develop political support, manage the transition, and sustain momentum during the change. For more on implementing change, see the next section.

Opposition to Organizational Changes

A manager designs his or her change effort, and then faces the toughest step: the inevitable opposition. History shows that workers have resisted some of the best-laid plans. A few may openly fight it. Many more may ignore or try to sabotage a manager's plan.

In the corporate world, most people, most of the time, resist change. Why? These people believe that change has very little upside for them—in other words, that change is rarely for the better.

One kind of resistance involves employees who have been with a company for a few years, and have seen flavor-of-the-month change programs come and go: Management launches some kind of change effort to great fanfare. Managers talk up the benefits and explain why this program will be good for both the company and its employees. They make promises, but at the end of the day, they fail to deliver. Nothing really happens, and the whole effort seems like a waste of time. Well, it makes sense to resist things that are a pure waste of time.

Another scenario: A number of consultants analyze a corporate department consisting of 100 people, and they conclude that the company needs just 48 of these people to complete the same amount of work. When an employee in this department learns of the consultants' recommendation, he or she fears being fired or working longer hours.

These kinds of dismal scenarios give employees the impression that change is not good. And employees have no reason to believe that it's going to be better in the future.

Here are some of the most common reasons employees resist change:

■ Uncertainty and insecurity

■ Reaction against the way change is presented

■ Threats to vested interests

■ Cynicism and lack of trust

■ Perceptual differences and lack of understanding

To overcome resistance, managers can involve workers in the change process by communicating openly about changes, providing advance notice of an upcoming change, exercising sensitivity to workers' concerns, and reassuring workers that change will not affect their security.

In addition, managers are more likely to implement changes successfully if they avoid common pitfalls that cause changes to fail. Some of these pitfalls are as follows:

■ Faulty thinking

■ Inadequate change process

■ Insufficient resources

■ Lack of commitment to change

■ Poor timing

■ A culture resistant to change

Steps for overcoming opposition

To implement planned change effectively, managers must understand how to overcome resistance to change, why change efforts fail, and what techniques they can use to modify behavior. Managers can use two approaches to change attitudes and behaviors at the individual level: the three-step approach and force-field analysis (the latter is discussed in the following section).

The process of change has been characterized as having three basic stages: unfreezing, changing, and refreezing.

1. **Unfreezing.** This step involves developing an initial awareness of the need for change and the forces supporting and resisting change. Because most people and organizations prefer stability and the perpetuation of the status quo, a successful change process must overcome the status quo by unfreezing old behaviors, processes, or structure. This approach includes the use of one-on-one discussions, presentations to groups, memos, reports, company newsletters, training programs, and demonstrations to educate employees about an imminent change and help them see the logic of the decision. Deficiencies in the current situation are identified and the benefits of the replacement are stressed.

2. **Changing.** This step focuses on learning new behaviors. Change results from individuals being uncomfortable with the identified negative behaviors and being presented with new behaviors, role models, and support. In this phase, something new takes place in a system, and change is actually implemented. This is the point at which managers initiate change in such organizational targets of tasks, people, culture, technology, and structure. When managers implement change, people must be ready.

3. **Refreezing** is the final stage. Refreezing centers on reinforcing new behaviors, usually by positive results, feelings of accomplishment, or rewards. After management has implemented changes in organizational goals, products, processes, structures, or people, they cannot sit back and expect the change to be maintained over time. Behaviors that are positively reinforced tend to be repeated. In designing change, attention must be paid to how the new behaviors will be reinforced and rewarded.

Force-field analysis

One of the earliest and most fundamental models of change, the Force-Field Analytic Problem-Solving Model, was developed by behavioral scientist Kurt Lewin in the 1940s. Since that time, this model has been widely used as a technique for encouraging groups of people to tackle organizational issues that previously seemed too complex or too deeply rooted to approach.

Force-field analysis depicts the change process as one that must overcome a person's or organization's status quo or existing state of equilibrium—the balance between forces for change and forces that resist change. In any problem situation, the existing condition (status quo) has been reached because of a number of opposing forces. The change forces are known as *drivers*. (Drivers push toward a solution to the problem.) Other forces are known as *resisters*. (Resisters inhibit improvement or solution of the problem.) When the strength of the drivers is approximately equal to the strength of the resisters, a balance or status quo is apparent. Until the relative strength of the forces is changed, the problem will continue to persist.

When a change is introduced, some forces drive it and other forces resist it. To implement a change, management should analyze the change forces. By selectively removing forces that resist change, the driving forces will be strong enough to enable implementation. As resistant forces are reduced or removed, behavior will shift to incorporate the desired changes.

To apply the model to a problem, a manager should follow these steps:

1. **Carefully and fully specify the problem (status quo).** A problem may be defined as the difference between what currently exists and what should exist.

2. **Define objectives.** A manager must consider what the situation will be like when it's solved.

3. **Brainstorm to determine the driving and resisting forces that contribute to the problem.**

4. **Analyze these forces more fully and develop a strategy.** This strategy should be aimed at strengthening the driving forces under a manager's control and weakening the resisting forces that a manager can realistically do something about.

5. **Compare strategy against company or departmental objectives.** A manager must consider whether his or her problem-solving strategy will promote a change in the status quo.

Organizational culture changes

Culture and people change in an organization refers to a shift in employees' values, norms, attitudes, beliefs, and behavior. Changes in culture and people pertain to how employees think; they're changes in mind-set rather than technology, structure, or products. *People change* pertains to just a few employees, such as when a handful of middle managers are sent to a training course to improve their leadership skills. *Culture change* pertains to the organization as a whole, such as changing an organization from a bureaucratic structure to a more participatory environment which focuses on employees providing customer service and quality through teamwork and employee participation.

An organization's values—what it holds to be important—are reflected in its culture. A manager's role is to ensure that the appropriate values are promoted, creating a positive organizational culture. The result is a thriving work environment with happy, motivated, and productive employees.

If managers want to take stock of their organizational culture, they should take the following steps:

1. **Identify the values that currently exist.**
2. **Determine whether these values are the right ones for your organization.**
3. **Change the actions and behaviors by which these values are demonstrated.**

If a manger doesn't like the values discovered in step two, he or she does have options. For example, managers may opt to take training courses to learn to improve their leadership skills, therefore effectively determining how to modify their employees' actions and behaviors (step three). If a manager finds that the organizational culture as a whole needs changing, a company may offer training programs to large blocks of employees on subjects such as teamwork, listening skills, and participative management.

A major approach to changing people and culture is through organizational development. Devoted to large-scale organizational change, **organizational development** (OD) focuses primarily on people processes as the target of change. Organizational development is grounded largely in psychology and other behavioral sciences, although more recently it has evolved into a broader approach encompassing such areas as organizational theory, strategy development, and social and technical change.

Used to create long-term policies for ongoing change, this approach applies behavioral science knowledge to the planned development of organizational strategies. Its goal is to change people and the quality of their interpersonal relationships. The aims of organizational development are as follows:

- Encourage cooperation

- Eliminate conflict

- Increase motivation

- Improve problem solving

- Open lines of communication

- Develop mutual trust

Popular organizational development tools consist of consultants, surveys, group discussion, and training sessions. Here's a brief description of some of the more common techniques used at these meetings:

- **Sensitivity training** is a method of changing behavior through unstructured group interaction.

- **Survey feedback** is a technique for assessing attitudes, identifying discrepancies in them, and resolving the differences by using survey information in feedback groups.

- **Process consultation** involves help given by an outside consultant to a manager in perceiving, understanding, and acting upon interpersonal processes.

- **Team building** includes interaction among members of work teams to learn how each member thinks and works.

- **Intergroup development** involves changing the attitudes, stereotypes, and perceptions that work groups have of each other.

So how do managers know whether OD is working effectively within their organizations? The primary evaluation of effectiveness uses the goals established when OD efforts and strategies began. Based on this evaluation, a manager can identify programs, strategies, and change agents that need to be redirected or improved.

Chapter Checkout

Q&A

1. The first step in the process of planned change is
   a. develop the goal(s).
   b. recognize the need for change.
   c. diagnose the problem.
   d. select the method of intervention.

2. Management consultant Larry Greiner contends that it takes a(n) _____ for an organization to evolve to the next phase of growth.
   a. crisis
   b. opportunity
   c. loss of sales
   d. merge with another company

3. The bridge of _____ separates people from change.
   a. acceptance
   b. resistance
   c. economics
   d. opportunity

4. Before a new established behavior can take place, the previous behavior(s) must be.
   a. forgotten and retrained.
   b. unfrozen and completed.
   c. thawed and changed.
   d. frozen and unfrozen.

5. A management technique for instituting change by thoroughly analyzing problems and implementing long-term solutions is known as
   a. management by objectives.
   b. creative management.
   c. organizational development.
   d. occupational management.

Answers: 1. b **2.** a **3.** b **4.** c **5.** c

Chapter 9

STAFFING AND HUMAN RESOURCE MANAGEMENT

Chapter Check-In

❏ Understanding the constraints on human resource management practices

❏ Determining an organization's staffing needs

❏ Finding, hiring, and training employees

❏ Evaluating and compensating employee performance

After an organization's structural design is in place, it needs people with the right skills, knowledge, and abilities to fill in that structure. People are an organization's most important resource, because people either create or undermine an organization's reputation for quality in both products and service.

In addition, an organization must respond to change effectively in order to remain competitive. The right staff can carry an organization through a period of change and ensure its future success. Because of the importance of hiring and maintaining a committed and competent staff, effective human resource management is crucial to the success of all organizations.

Attracting, developing, rewarding, and retraining the people needed to reach organizational goals are the activities that make up the staffing function. This chapter discusses each of these activities, as well as the laws that impact all areas of staffing.

Staffing as a Management Function

Human resource management (HRM), or *staffing*, is the management function devoted to acquiring, training, appraising, and compensating employees. In effect, all managers are human resource managers, although human resource specialists may perform some of these activities in large organizations. Solid HRM practices can mold a company's workforce into a motivated and committed team capable of managing change effectively and achieving the organizational objectives.

Understanding the fundamentals of HRM can help any manager lead more effectively. Every manager should understand the following three principles:

- All managers are human resource managers.

- Employees are much more important assets than buildings or equipment; good employees give a company the competitive edge.

- Human resource management is a matching process; it must match the needs of the organization with the needs of the employee.

Laws and Regulations Affecting HRM

Laws and regulations at the federal, state, and local levels regulate how companies conduct staffing. Title VII of the 1964 Civil Rights Act banned most discriminatory hiring practices.

Three sensitive areas of legal concern that managers must comply with are equal opportunity, affirmative action, and sexual harassment, described in the following sections. These areas, as well as other laws, impact all human resource practices.

Equal Employment Opportunity

Individuals covered under Equal Employment Opportunity (EEO) laws are protected from illegal discrimination, which occurs when people who share a certain characteristic, such as race, age, or gender, are discriminated against because of that characteristic. People who have the designated characteristics are called the *protected class*. Federal laws have identified the following characteristics for protection:

- Race, ethnic origin, color (for example, African American, Hispanic, Native American, Asian)

- Gender (women, including those who are pregnant)

- Age (individuals over 40)

- Individuals with disabilities (physical and mental)

- Military experience (Vietnam-era veterans)
- Religion (special beliefs and practices)

The main purpose of the EEO laws is to ensure that everyone has an equal opportunity of getting a job or being promoted at work.

Affirmative action

While EEO laws aim to ensure equal treatment at work, **affirmative action** requires the employer to make an extra effort to hire and promote people who belong to a protected group. Affirmative action includes taking specific actions designed to eliminate the present effects of past discriminations.

Employees are also protected by the **Equal Employment Opportunity Commission (EEOC),** which was established through the 1964 Civil Rights Act, Title VII. The scope of authority of the EEOC has been expanded so that today it carries the major enforcement authority for the following laws:

- **Civil Rights Act of 1964.** Prohibits discrimination on the basis of race, color, religion, national origin, or sex.

- **Civil Rights Act of 1991.** Reaffirms and tightens prohibition of discrimination. Permits individuals to sue for punitive damages in cases of intentional discrimination and shifts the burden of proof to the employer.

- **Equal Pay Act of 1963.** Prohibits pay differences based on sex for equal work.

- **Pregnancy Discrimination Act of 1978.** Prohibits discrimination or dismissal of women because of pregnancy alone, and protects job security during maternity leaves.

- **Americans with Disabilities Act.** Prohibits discrimination against individuals with physical or mental disabilities or the chronically ill, and requires that "reasonable accommodations" be provided for the disabled.

- **Vocational Rehabilitation Act.** Prohibits discrimination on the basis of physical or mental disabilities and requires that employees be informed about affirmative action plans.

Most employers in the United States must comply with the provisions of Title VII. Compliance is required from all private employers of 15 or more persons, all educational institutions, state and local governments, public and private employment agencies, labor unions with 15 or more members, and joint (labor-management) committees for apprenticeship and training.

Sexual harassment

Few workplace topics have received more attention in recent years than that of sexual harassment. Since professor Anita Hill confronted Supreme Court nominee Clarence Thomas on national television over a decade ago, the number of sexual harassment claims filed annually in the United States has more than doubled.

Since 1980, U.S. courts generally have used guidelines from the Equal Employment Opportunity Commission to define sexual harassment. *Sexual harassment* is defined as "unwelcome sexual advances for sexual favors, and other verbal or physical conduct of a sexual nature." Sexual harassment may include sexually suggestive remarks, unwanted touching, sexual advances, requests for sexual favors, and other verbal and physical conduct of a sexual nature

In a 1993 ruling, the Supreme Court widened the test for sexual harassment under the civil rights law to whether comments or behavior in a work environment "would reasonably be perceived, and is perceived as hostile or abusive." As a result, employees don't need to demonstrate that they have been psychologically damaged to prove sexual harassment in the workplace; they simply must prove that they are working in a hostile or abusive environment.

Sexual harassment is not just a woman's problem. Recently, a decision handed down by the U.S. Supreme Court broadened the definition of sexual harassment to include same-sex harassment as well as harassment of males by female coworkers. In the suit that prompted the Court's decision, a male oil-rig worker claimed he was singled out by other members of the all-male crew for crude sex play, unwanted touching, and threats.

From management's standpoint, sexual harassment is a growing concern because it intimidates employees, interferes with job performance, and exposes the organization to liability. Organizations must respond to sexual harassment complaints very quickly because employers are held responsible for sexual harassment if appropriate action is not taken. The cost of inaction can be high. The Civil Rights Act of 1991 permits victims of sexual harassment to have jury trials and to collect compensatory damages in cases where the employer acted with "malice or reckless indifference" to the individual's rights.

Employers can take the following steps to help minimize liability for sexual harassment suits:

1. **Offer a sexual harassment policy statement.** This statement should address where employees can report complaints, assure confidentiality, and promise that disciplinary action will be taken against sexual harassers.

2. **Provide communication and training programs for supervisors and managers.** These programs should emphasize that sexual harassment will not be tolerated.

3. **Conduct fair, impartial investigations and base actions on objectively gathered facts.** The complainant must be insulated from the kinds of behavior that prompted the complaint.

Other employment laws

Several other laws impact staffing practices as well. The Fair Labor Standards Act specifies the minimum wage, overtime pay rules, and child labor regulations. The Employee Polygraph Protection Act outlaws almost all uses of the polygraph machine for employment purposes. Privacy laws provide legal rights regarding who has access to information about work history and job performance for employees in certain jurisdictions. Under the Whistleblower Protection Act, some employees who publicize dangerous employer practices are entitled to legal protection. Table 9-1 lists additional federal laws that shape HRM practices.

Table 9-1   Some Federal Laws Shaping HRM Practices

Law	Date	Description
National Labor Relations Act	1935	Requires employers to recognize a union chosen by the majority of the employees and to establish procedures governing collective bargaining.
Age Discrimination in Employment Act	1967, amended in 1978 and 1986	Prohibits age discrimination against employees between 40 and 65 years of age and restricts mandatory retirement.

Law	Date	Description
Occupational Safety and Health Act	1970	Establishes mandatory safety and health standards in organizations.
Vietnam-Era Veteran's Readjustment Assistance Act	1974	Prohibits discrimination against disabled veterans and Vietnam-era veterans.
Mandatory Retirement Act	1978	Prohibits the forced retirement of most employees before the age of 70.
Immigration Reform and Control Act	1986	Prohibits employers from knowingly hiring illegal aliens and prohibits employment on the basis of national origin of citizenship.
Worker Adjustment and Retraining Notification Act	1988	Requires employees to provide 60 days' notice before a facility closing or mass layoff.
Employee Polygraph Protection Act	1988	Limits an employer's ability to use lie detector tests.
Family and Medical Leave Act	1993	Permits employees in organizations with 50 or more workers to take up to 12 weeks of unpaid leave for family or medical reasons for each year.

Determining Human Resource Needs

Staffing is an ongoing process that begins with finding the right people through proper planning, recruiting, and selecting. But staffing doesn't end once employees are hired; management must keep and nurture its people via training, appraising, compensating, and implementing employment decisions that determine such things as promotions, transfers, and layoffs.

Human resource planning

The first step in the staffing process involves human resource planning. Human resource planning begins with a **job analysis** in which descriptions of all jobs (tasks) and the qualifications needed for each position are developed. A **job description** is a written statement of what a jobholder does, how it's done, and why it's done. It typically portrays job content, environment, and conditions of employment. The job specification states the minimum acceptable qualifications an incumbent must possess to perform a given job successfully. It identifies the knowledge, skills, and abilities needed to do the job effectively.

Job analysis is then followed by a human resource inventory, which catalogs qualifications and interests. Next, a human resource forecast is developed to predict the organization's future needs for jobs and people based on its strategic plans and normal attrition. The forecast is then compared to the inventory to determine whether the organization's staffing needs will be met with existing personnel or whether managers will have to recruit new employees or terminate existing ones.

Recruiting strategies

Recruitment includes all the activities an organization may use to attract a pool of viable candidates. Effective recruiting is increasingly important today for several reasons:

- The U.S. employment rate has generally declined each year through the 1990s. Experts refer to the current recruiting situation as one of "evaporated employee resources."

- Many experts believe that today's Generation X employees (those born between 1963 and 1981) are less inclined to build long-term employment relationships than were their predecessors. Therefore, finding the right inducements for attracting, hiring, and retaining qualified personnel may be more complicated than in previous years.

Keep in mind that recruiting strategies differ among organizations. Although one may instantly think of campus recruiting as a typical recruiting activity, many organizations use internal recruiting, or promote-from-within policies, to fill their high-level positions. Open positions are posted, and current employees are given preferences when these positions become available. Internal recruitment is less costly than an external search. It also generates higher employee commitment, development, and satisfaction because it offers opportunities for career advancement to employees rather than outsiders.

If internal sources do not produce an acceptable candidate, many external recruiting strategies are available, including the following:

- Newspaper advertising

- Employment agencies (private, public, or temporary agencies)

- Executive recruiters (sometimes called headhunters)

- Unions

- Employee referrals

- Internship programs
- Internet employment sites

But there's more to recruiting than just attracting employees; managers need to be able to weed out the top candidates. Once a manger has a pool of applicants, the selection process can begin.

Selecting the Best Person for the Job

Having the right people on staff is crucial to the success of an organization. Various selection devices help employers predict which applicants will be successful if hired. These devices aim to be not only valid, but also reliable. *Validity* is proof that the relationship between the selection device and some relevant job criterion exists. *Reliability* is an indicator that the device measures the same thing consistently. For example, it would be appropriate to give a keyboarding test to a candidate applying for a job as an administrative assistant. However, it would not be valid to give a keyboarding test to a candidate for a job as a physical education teacher. If a keyboarding test is given to the same individual on two separate occasions, the results should be similar. To be effective predictors, a selection device must possess an acceptable level of consistency.

Application forms

For most employers, the application form is the first step in the selection process. Application forms provide a record of salient information about applicants for positions, and also furnish data for personnel research. Interviewers may use responses from the application for follow-up questions during an interview.

These forms range from requests for basic information, such as names, addresses, and telephone numbers, to comprehensive personal history profiles detailing applicants' education, job experience skills, and accomplishments.

According to the Uniform Selection Guidelines of the EEOC, which establish standards that employers must meet to prevent disparate or unequal treatment, any employment requirement is a test, even a job application. As a result, EEOC considerations and application forms are interrelated, and managers should make sure that their application forms do not ask questions that are irrelevant to job success, or these questions may create an adverse impact on protected groups.

For example, employers should not ask whether an applicant rents or owns his or her own home, because an applicant's response may adversely affect his or her chances at the job. Minorities and women may be less likely to own a home, and home ownership is probably unrelated to job performance.

On the other hand, asking about the CPA exam for an accounting position is appropriate, even if only one-half of all female or minority applicants have taken the exam versus nine-tenths of male applicants.

A quick test for disparate impact suggested by the Uniform Selection Guidelines is the **four-fifths rules.** Generally, a disparate impact is assumed when the proportions of protected class applicants who are actually hired is less that 80 percent (four-fifths) of the proportion of the majority group applicants selected. For example, assume that an employer has 100 white male applicants for an entry-level job and hires one-half of them, for a selection ratio of 1:2, or 50 percent (50/100). The four-fifths rule does not mean that the employers must hire four-fifths, or 40 protected class members. Instead, the rule means that the employer's selection ratio of protected class-applicants should be at least four-fifths of that of the majority groups.

Testing

Testing is another method of selecting competent future employees. Although testing use has ebbed and flowed during the past two decades, recent studies reveal that more than 80 percent of employers use testing as part of their selection process.

Again, these tests must be valid and reliable, or serious EEO questions may be raised about the use of them. As a result, a manager needs to make sure that the test measures only job-relevant dimensions of applicants.

Most tests focus on specific job-related aptitudes and skills, such as math or motor skills. Typical types of exams include the following:

- **Integrity tests** measure factors such as dependability, carefulness, responsibility, and honesty. These tests are used to learn about the attitudes of applicants toward a variety of job-related subjects. Since the passage of the Employee Polygraph Protection Act in 1988, polygraph (lie detector) tests have been effectively banned in employment situations. In their place, attitude tests are being used to assess attitudes about honesty and, presumably, on-the-job behaviors.

- **Personality tests** measure personality or temperament. These tests are among the least reliable. Personality tests are problematic and not very valid, because little or no relationship exists between personality and performance.

■ **Knowledge tests** are more reliable than personality tests because they measure an applicant's comprehension or knowledge of a subject. A math test for an accountant and a weather test for a pilot are examples. Human relations specialists must be able to demonstrate that the test reflects the knowledge needed to perform the job. For example, a teacher hired to teach math should not be given a keyboarding test.

■ **Performance simulation tests** are increasing in popularity. Based on job analysis data, they more easily meet the requirement of job relatedness than written tests. Performance simulation tests are made up of actual job behaviors. The best-known performance simulation test is known as work sampling, and other credible similation processes are performed at assessment centers.

■ An *assessment* is a selection technique that examines candidates' handling of simulated job situations and evaluates a candidate's potential by observing his or her performance in experiential activities designed to simulate daily work.

> **Assessment centers,** where work sampling is often completed, utilize line executives, supervisors, or trained psychologists to evaluate candidates as they go through exercises that simulate real problems that these candidates would confront on their jobs. Activities may include interviews, problem-solving exercises, group discussions, and business-decision games. Assessment centers have consistently demonstrated results that accurately predict later job performance in managerial positions.

> **Work sampling** is an effort to create a miniature replica of a job, giving applicants the chance to demonstrate that they possess the necessary talents by actually doing the tasks.

Interviews

Another widely used selection technique is the *interview,* a formal, in-depth conversation conducted to evaluate an applicant's acceptability. In general, the interviewer seeks to answer three broad questions:

1. Can the applicant do the job?
2. Will the applicant do the job?
3. How does the applicant compare with others who are being considered for the job?

Interviews are popular because of their flexibility. They can be adapted to unskilled, skilled, managerial, and staff employees. They also allow a two-way exchange of information where interviewers can learn about the applicant and the applicant can learn about the employer.

Interviews do have some shortcomings, however. The most noticeable flaws are in the areas of reliability and validity. Good reliability means that the interpretation of the interview results does not vary from interviewer to interviewer. Reliability is improved when identical questions are asked. The validity of interviews is often questionable because few departments use standardized questions.

Managers can boost the reliability and validity of selection interviews by planning the interviews, establishing rapport, closing the interview with time for questions, and reviewing the interview as soon as possible after its conclusion.

Other selection techniques

Reference checking and health exams are two other important selection techniques that help in the staffing decision.

- **Reference checking** allows employers to verify information supplied by the candidate. However, obtaining information about potential candidates is often difficult because of privacy laws and employer concerns about defamation lawsuits.

- **Health exams** identify health problems that increase absenteeism and accidents, as well as detecting diseases that may be unknown to the applicant.

Orientation and Training Programs

Once employees are selected, they must be prepared to do their jobs, which is when orientation and training come in. **Orientation** means providing new employees with basic information about the employer. Training programs are used to ensure that the new employee has the basic knowledge required to perform the job satisfactorily.

Orientation and training programs are important components in the processes of developing a committed and flexible high-potential workforce and socializing new employees. In addition, these programs can save employers money, providing big returns to an organization, because an organization that invests money to train its employees results in both the employees and the organization enjoying the dividends.

Unfortunately, orientation and training programs are often overlooked. A recent U.S. study, for example, found that 57 percent of employers reported that although employees' skill requirements had increased over a three-year period, only 20 percent of employees were fully proficient in their jobs.

Orientation

Orientation programs not only improve the rate at which employees are able to perform their jobs but also help employees satisfy their personal desires to feel they are part of the organization's social fabric. The HR department generally orients newcomers to broad organizational issues and fringe benefits. Supervisors complete the orientation process by introducing new employees to coworkers and others involved in the job. A buddy or mentor may be assigned to continue the process.

Training needs

Simply hiring and placing employees in jobs does not ensure their success. In fact, even tenured employees may need training, because of changes in the business environment. Here are some changes that may signal that current employees need training:

- Introduction of new equipment or processes

- A change in the employee's job responsibilities

- A drop in an employee's productivity or in the quality of output

- An increase in safety violations or accidents

- An increased number of questions

- Complaints by customers or coworkers

Once managers decide that their employees need training, these managers need to develop clear training goals that outline anticipated results. These managers must also be able to clearly communicate these goals to employees.

Keep in mind that training is only one response to a performance problem. If the problem is lack of motivation, a poorly designed job, or an external condition (such as a family problem), training is not likely to offer much help.

Types of training

After specific training goals have been established, training sessions should be scheduled to provide the employee an opportunity to meet his or her goals. The following are typical training programs provided by employers:

- **Basic literacy training.** Ninety million American adults have limited literacy skills, and about 40 million can read little or not at all. Because most workplace demands require a tenth- or eleventh-grade reading level (and about 20 percent of Americans between the ages of 21 and 25 can't read at even an eighth-grade level), organizations increasingly need to provide basic literacy training in the areas of reading and math skills to their employees.

- **Technical training.** New technology and structural designs have increased the need to upgrade and improve employees' technical skills in both white-collar and blue-collar jobs.

- **Interpersonal skills training.** Most employees belong to a work team, and their work performance depends on their abilities to effectively interact with their coworkers. Interpersonal skills training helps employees build communication skills.

- **Problem-solving training.** Today's employees often work as members of self-managed teams who are responsible for solving their own problems. Problem-solving training has become a basic part of almost every organizational effort to introduce self-managed teams or implement Total Quality Management (TQM). (Chapter 15 is devoted to TQM.)

- **Diversity training.** As one of the fastest growing areas of training, diversity training increases awareness and builds cultural sensitivity skills. Awareness training tries to create an understanding of the need for, and meaning of, managing and valuing diversity. Skill-building training educates employees about specific cultural differences in the workplace.

Training methods

Most training takes place on the job due to the simplicity and lower cost of **on-the-job** training methods. Two popular types of on-the-job training include the following:

- **Job rotation.** By assigning people to different jobs or tasks to different people on a temporary basis, employers can add variety and expose people to the dependence that one job has on others. Job rotation can help stimulate people to higher levels of contributions, renew people's interest and enthusiasm, and encourage them to work more as a team.

- **Mentoring programs.** A new employee frequently learns his or her job under the guidance of a seasoned veteran. In the trades, this type of training is usually called an apprenticeship. In white-collar jobs, it is called a coaching or mentoring relationship. In each, the new employee works under the observation of an experienced worker.

Sometimes, training goals cannot be met through on-the-job training; the employer needs to look to other resources. *Off-the-job training* can rely on outside consultants, local college faculty, or in-house personnel. The more popular off-the-job training methods are classroom lectures, videos, and simulation exercises. Thanks to new technologies, employers can now facilitate some training, such as tutorials, on the employees' own computers, reducing the overall costs.

Regardless of the method selected, effective training should be individualized. Some people absorb information better when they read about it, others learn best by observation, and still others learn better when they hear the information. These different learning styles are not mutually exclusive. When training is designed around the preferred learning style of an employee, the benefits of training are maximized because employees are able to retain more of what they learn.

In addition to training, employers should offer **development plans,** which include a series of steps that can help employees acquire skills to reach long-term goals, such as a job promotion. Training, on the other hand, is immediate and specific to a current job.

Evaluating Employee Performance

Employee performance should be evaluated regularly. Employees want feedback—they want to know what their supervisors think about their work. Regular performance evaluations not only provide feedback to employees, but also provide employees with an opportunity to correct deficiencies. Evaluations or reviews also help in making key personnel decisions, such as the following:

- Justifying promotions, transfers, and terminations
- Identifying training needs
- Providing feedback to employees on their performance
- Determining necessary pay adjustments

Most organizations utilize employee evaluation systems; one such system is known as a **performance appraisal.** A performance appraisal is a formal, structured system designed to measure the actual job performance of an employee against designated performance standards. Although performance appraisals systems vary by organizations, all employee evaluations should have the following three components:

■ Specific, job-related criteria against which performance can be compared

■ A rating scale that lets employees know how well they're meeting the criteria

■ Objective methods, forms, and procedures to determine the rating

Traditionally, an employee's immediate boss conducts his or her performance appraisal. However, some organizations use other devices, such as peer evaluations, self-appraisals, and even customer evaluations, for conducting this important task.

The latest approach to performance evaluation is the use of 360-degree feedback. The *360-degree feedback appraisal* provides performance feedback from the full circle of daily contacts that an employee may have. This method of performance appraisal fits well into organizations that have introduced teams, employee involvement, and TQM programs.

Making Employment Decisions

Employment decisions go beyond determining which employees are due for raises. Through regular, objective performance appraisals, managers acquire information to make and implement decisions about promotions, transfers, demotions, separations, and compensation.

In most organizations, outstanding employees are recognized for their hard work and outstanding performances, and offered promotions. A promotion generally means rewarding an employee's efforts by moving that person to a job with increased authority and responsibility.

Downsizing has led many firms to rely on lateral moves or transfers instead of promoting employees. A lateral move can act as an opportunity for future vertical advancement because it can broaden an employee's experiences and add skills.

On the other hand, sometimes employees' performances signal that they aren't adapting well to their jobs and may need fewer responsibilities. One option is a demotion, or reassignment to a lower rank or less prestigious position. Demotions are not a popular technique because of the stigma attached to this move. A misconception is that demotions should be used as punishment for ineffective performance.

The departure of an employee from an organization is referred to as separation. Separation may be voluntary or involuntary. Resignations and retirements are voluntary separations. Involuntary separations are layoffs and/or firings. Lately, the rash of downsizing throughout the United States has resulted in many layoffs.

Sometimes, however, an employee must be terminated because of poor performance. Dismissal or firing of employees should occur only on the basis of just cause and only after all reasonable steps to rehabilitate the employee have failed. In some cases, such as gross insubordination or theft, immediate dismissal is required.

Compensating Employees

Employee **compensation** refers to all work-related payments, including wages, commissions, insurance, and time off.

Wages and salaries are the most obvious forms of compensation and are based on job evaluations that determine the relative values of jobs to the organization. Under the hourly wage system, employees are paid a fixed amount for each hour they work. The system is generally used for lower skilled occupations. Salaried employees receive a fixed sum per week or month, no matter how many hours they work. Most professional positions are salaried; the reality is that these jobholders typically work in excess of a "minimum" 40-hour workweek.

Some occupations are compensated through incentive pay programs. Salespeople typically receive commissions based upon the quantities of goods they sell. Some sales compensation plans contain elements of both a salary and commission. A production worker's pay may be based upon some combination of an hourly wage and an incentive for each "piece" he or she makes. Some employees are offered merit awards as a reward for sustained superior performance.

Employee benefits are supplements to wages or pay. Some benefits, such as unemployment and worker's compensation, are legally mandated. Other benefits are optional and help build employee loyalty to an organization, including the following:

■ Health insurance

■ Pension plans

■ Employee discounts

■ Vacation, sick, and personal days

■ Bonuses (incentive money paid to employees in addition to their regular compensation)

■ Profit-sharing (money from a portion of the company profits used to supplement regular compensation)

■ Stock options (a plan that permits employees to buy shares of stock in the employee's firm at or below the present market value)

A top management executive is given benefits unique to his or her status. Additional executive benefits are termed perquisites (perks).

Chapter Checkout

Q&A

1. The primary purposes of staffing include all of the following except
   a. disciplining employees.
   b. finding employees.
   c. hiring employees.
   d. rewarding employees.

2. Affirmative action is defined as
   a. any employment decision that harms one individual more than any other.
   b. any employment decision that is based upon sexual conduct.
   c. a law that requires employers to make an extra effort to employ protected groups.
   d. any employment decision that harms one group more than another.

3. An in-depth study of all the positions in an organization is described as a

   a. job evaluation.

   b. job description.

   c. job analysis.

   d. job specification.

4. Any criterion of performance measure used as a basis for an employment decision is a(n)

   a. assessment center.

   b. performance standard.

   c. test.

   d. None of the above.

5. All of the following would be considered a separation except a(n)

   a. demotion.

   b. layoff.

   c. retirement.

   d. firing.

Answers: 1. a **2.** c **3.** c **4.** c **5.** a

Chapter 10

UNDERSTANDING TEAMS

Chapter Check-In

❑ Building and managing effective teams

❑ Understanding the stages of team development

❑ Overcoming team discord

As part of a team, an employee is required to give his or her all for the team, professionally speaking. Ideally, working toward a common goal should be the most important reward for any employee. And as a team member, an employee should be proud and motivated to be a part of the team's effort toward organizational goals. When a team achieves a goal, each team member is unlikely to forget his or her experience of being a part of a successful team.

In the new world of business, many tasks are completed through teamwork, but very few teams work all that well. In this chapter, methods ordinary team members can use to achieve extraordinary results are discussed. Also examined in this chapter are the different types of work teams, the stages of team development, the benefits of teams, and the strategies that management can use to resolve team conflicts.

Teamwork Defined

The traditional workplace, with its emphasis on internal competition and individual star performers, is undergoing a transformation. In U.S. businesses, a strong movement toward the use of teams is occurring. Management experts and researchers suggest that a successful organization is characterized by effective teamwork and leadership rather than management. Organizations are realizing the importance of developing teams that can work in a coordinated, efficient, and creative manner.

As a result, managers are responsible for creating, developing, and supporting the cooperative efforts of individuals under their influence. Compiling honest, clear-eyed evaluations of how these individuals interact is a critical first step to building cohesive, long-term working relationships. Interactions among employees can be characterized in three ways:

- **Groups:** A group exists almost anywhere two or more people interact or coexist. A group does not have a unified purpose. Many people mistakenly expect that simply working in close proximity to others is enough to allow an effective team to emerge. Not so. Although individuals may be close physically, don't assume that their thought processes or levels of commitment are in sync. Remember that an individual may work simply for a paycheck and exhibit a lack of concern for the organization, its activities, its mission, and its people that is obvious to even the most casual observer. These individuals do just enough to get by, but not enough to make a difference.

- **Mobs:** Unlike groups, mobs have a unified purpose. Mobs of employees often form with the focused intent to challenge, malign, or even sabotage the established order. Although many people think of mobs as chaotic, disorganized, and unstructured, they are actually very purposeful in their actions.

- **Team:** Teams share a common goal. A team is composed of two or more people who interact regularly and coordinate their work to accomplish a mutual objective. Some management experts believe that highest productivity results only when groups become teams.

The major difference between groups and teams centers around how work gets done. Work groups emphasize individual work products, individual accountability, and even individual-centered leadership. In contrast, work teams share leadership roles, have both individual and mutual accountability, and create collective work products. In other words, a work group's performance is a function of what its members do as individuals, while a team's performance is based on collective results—what two or more workers accomplish jointly.

Types of Teams

The development of teams and teamwork has grown dramatically in all types of organizations for one simple reason: No one person has the ability to deliver the kinds of products and services required in today's highly competitive marketplace. Organizations must depend on the cooperative nature of many teams to create successful ventures and outcomes.

Teams can be vertical (functional), horizontal (cross-functional), or self-directed (self-managed) and can be used to create new products, complete specific projects, ensure quality, or replace operating departments.

- **Functional teams** perform specific organizational functions and include members from several vertical levels of the hierarchy. In other words, a functional team is composed of a manager and his or her subordinates for a particular functional area. Accounting, personnel, and purchasing departments are examples of functional teams.

- **Cross-functional teams** are made up of experts in various specialties (or functions) working together on various organizational tasks. Team members come from such departments as research and development, design, engineering, marketing, and distribution. These teams are often empowered to make decisions without the approval of management. For example, when Nabisco's executives concluded that the company needed to improve its relationship with customers and better satisfy customers' needs, they created cross-functional teams whose assignments were to find ways to do just that. Although functional teams are usually permanent, cross-functional teams are often temporary, lasting for as little as a few months or as long as several years, depending on the group tasks being performed.

- **Self-directed work teams,** or self-managed teams, operate without managers and are responsible for complete work processes or segments that deliver products or services to external or internal customers. Self-directed work teams (SDWTs) are designed to give employees a feeling of "ownership" of a whole job. For example, at Tennessee Eastman, a division of Eastman Kodak Company, teams are responsible for whole product lines—including processing, lab work, and packaging. With shared team responsibilities for work outcomes, team members often have broader job assignments and cross-train to master other jobs. This cross-training permits greater team flexibility.

No matter what type of team is formed, the benefits of teamwork are many, including synergy and increased skills, knowledge, productivity, flexibility, and commitment. Among the other benefits are increased job satisfaction, employee empowerment, and improved quality and organizational effectiveness.

Effectiveness of Teams

High-performance teams don't just appear; they are developed and nurtured. By themselves, leaders with vision cannot guarantee the development of such high-performance teams, nor can members who desire to be part of such teams. The development of high-performance teams takes the combined efforts of visionary leaders and motivated team members. In addition, facilitators with expertise in team building are needed. The following lists the characteristics that comprise high-performance teams:

- The team has a common focus, including clear and understandable goals, plans of action, and ways to measure success.

- Roles and responsibilities are clearly defined for each team member.

- Each member has clearly defined expectations of other members.

- The team fully utilizes its resources—both internal and external.

- Members value each other's differences in healthy and productive ways.

- Each member is able to give, receive, and elicit necessary feedback.

- The team members manage their meetings in a productive way.

- The team is able to reach goals by achieving the necessary results.

To build an effective team, a leader needs to establish an organizational environment in which individual team members can reflect upon and analyze relationships with other team members. A leader should encourage the resolution of any conflicts through healthy, professional confrontation, and willingly and openly negotiate necessary changes. In short, effective leaders are cheerleaders for the team; they encourage and support members who are committed and actively involved with their teams and engage those members who aren't participating.

Several factors within an organization itself influence team effectiveness, including its organizational culture, level of autonomy, and types of feedback mechanisms. But the factors that influence the effectiveness of a team most directly stem from its internal structure and processes.

- **Structural factors** include team or group type, size, and composition of skills and abilities.

- **Team processes** include stages of team development, cultural norms, roles cohesiveness, and interpersonal processes such as trust development, facilitation, influence, leadership communication, and conflict resolution.

To judge the effectiveness of their teams, leaders need to examine their teams' performances and personal outcomes. *Performance outcomes* may be measured by products made, ideas generated, customers served, numbers of defects per thousand items produced, overtime hours, items sold, and customer satisfaction levels. *Personal outcomes* may be measured by employee satisfaction, commitment, and willingness of members to stay on the team. Both outcomes are important for the long-term viability as well as the short-term success of the team.

Team Building

Team building requires managers to follow a systematic planning and implementation process to assess whether teams can improve the organization's goal attainment; to remove barriers to team building; and to build effective teams through training, empowerment, and feedback. Managers must also decide on team size and member roles to gain the maximum contribution for all members.

To create effective teams, managers need to avoid the following six deadly sins of team building:

1. **Lack of a model.** A team leader often focuses on a single aspect of team functioning, such as communication practices. But many other elements are critical to team success and effectiveness, and a team is only as strong as its weakest component. A single-dimensional team-building process may cause frustration and destroy the credibility of the process.

   Fix: A model of how teams function is needed to address all the factors that result in reduced team effectiveness. At a minimum, the following must be considered for team effectiveness:

   • Clearly stated and commonly held vision and goals

   • Talent and skills required to meet the goals

   • Clear understanding of team members' roles and functions

   • Efficient and shared understanding of procedures and norms

   • Effective and skilled interpersonal relations

   • A system of reinforcement and celebration

   • Clear understanding of the team's relationship to the organization

2. **Lack of diagnosis.** Each team has distinct strengths and weaknesses, which team building must take into account. The team leader must be aware of these strengths and weaknesses.

   Fix: The leader must assess his team's strength and weaknesses. Although assessment and diagnostic instruments can be purchased, hiring an outside consultant to complete a thorough team assessment is advisable.

3. **Short-term intervention.** Some managers think that a one-day retreat or team-building exercise will resolve issues causing tension and frustration. One day, no matter how good it is, is not going to make much of a change in the norms, culture, or practices of a team. A one-day retreat may bring to light issues that cannot be solved during that day and are left to fester, resulting in team members mistrusting the process.

   Fix: Plan a long-term strategy for team building. One year is a good time frame for this plan.

4. **No evaluation of progress.** Because team building is a long-term process, both management and team members need to know whether it is succeeding. A mechanism for regular evaluation of team functioning needs to be in place so that the team leader can identify barriers and eliminate them.

   Fix: Plan regular evaluations of team progress. The diagnostic instrument used initially can be used at regular intervals to gauge progress.

5. **Leadership detachment.** The detached manager looks at team development as something that will help others change so that the team will function more effectively. However, the most influential person in most teams is the formal leader or manager who sets the tone for the team, whether intentionally or unintentionally.

   Fix: A manager must be willing to hear from employees about how his or her behavior impacts the team, whether negatively or positively. The worst thing that an organization can do is to start the process and refuse to acknowledge that a manager is a key player in the process.

6. **Addressing all problems internally.** Team building cannot succeed unless conflicts and problems are brought into the open and dealt with properly. Poorly functioning teams are characterized by climates of blame, defensiveness, and a lack of ability to deal with conflict. These teams cannot improve themselves.

Fix: Consider hiring an outside consultant to help if a team is very negative or has unresolved conflicts. The most important reason for using an outside consultant is that an "outsider" has no preconceptions or agenda.

Remember that poor team building is worse than doing nothing. Poorly thought-out efforts are likely to increase negativity, reduce team functioning, and reduce management credibility. A manager's personal reputation and the degree to which employees have confidence in him or her are at stake.

Stages of Team Development

Because a work team is a common arrangement within today's business organizations, managers need to understand group behavior and team concepts. Team building requires a manager to follow a systematic planning and implementation process to assess whether his or her team can improve the organization's goal attainment; remove barriers to team building; and build an effective team through training, empowerment, and feedback. Managers must also decide on team size and member roles to gain the maximum contribution from all members.

Generally, when organizations form teams, these organizations have specific projects or goals in mind. A team is simply a tool that accomplishes a project or goal.

But no matter what the reason teams are formed, they go through four stages, according to a 1965 research paper by Bruce Tuckman of the Naval Medical Research Institute at Bethesda. The following sections describe Tuckman's four stages.

Stage 1: Forming

During the forming stage, team members not only get to know each other but also familiarize themselves with their task and with other individuals interested in the project, such as supervisors. At the end of the forming stage, team members should know the following:

■ The project's overall mission

■ The main phases of the mission

■ The resources at their disposal

■ A rough project schedule

- Each member's project responsibilities
- A basic set of team rules

Keep in mind that no one person needs to be responsible for the team. Project management duties can be shared, with different members taking responsibilities for each stage of the project.

Stage 2: Storming

Storming is characterized by competition and conflict within the team as members learn to bend and mold their feelings, ideas, attitudes, and beliefs to suit the team organization. Although conflicts may or may not surface as group issues, they do exist. Questions about who is responsible for what, what the rules are, what the reward system is, and what the evaluation criteria are arise. These questions reflect conflicts over leadership, structure, power, and authority. Because of the discomfort generated during this stage, some members may remain completely silent, while others attempt to dominate. Members have an increased desire for structural clarification and commitment.

In order to progress to the next stage, team members must move from a testing-and-proving mentality to a problem-solving mentality. Listening is the most helpful action team members and the team leader can take to resolve these issues.

Stage 3: Norming

In Tuckman's norming stage, team relations are characterized by cohesion. (Keep in mind that not all teams reach this stage.) Team members actively acknowledge all members' contributions, build community, maintain team focus and mission, and work to solve team issues. Members are willing to change their preconceived ideas or opinions on the basis of facts presented by other members, and they actively ask questions of one another. Leadership is shared, and cliques dissolve. As members begin to know and identify with one another, the trust that individuals place in their colleagues fosters cohesion within the team.

During this stage of development, team members begin to experience a sense of group belonging and a feeling of relief as a result of resolving interpersonal conflicts.

Stage 3 is characterized by the flow of data between team members: They share feelings and ideas, solicit and give feedback to one another, and explore actions related to the task. Creativity is high. If this stage of data flow and cohesion is attained by the group members, their interactions are characterized by openness and sharing of information on both a personal and task level. They feel good about being part of an effective group.

The major drawback of the norming stage is that members may begin to fear the inevitable future breakup of the group; they may resist change of any sort.

Stage 4: Performing

Again, the performing stage is not reached by all teams. Those teams that do reach this stage not only enjoy team members who work independently but also support those who can come back together and work interdependently to solve problems. A team is at its most productive during this stage.

Team members are both highly task-oriented and highly people-oriented during this stage. The team is unified: Team identity is complete, team morale is high, and team loyalty is intense. The task function becomes genuine problem solving, leading to optimal solutions and optimum team development. There is support for experimentation in solving problems, and an emphasis on achievement. The overall goal is productivity through problem solving and work.

Adjourning

Teams assembled for specific project or for a finite length of time go through a fifth stage, called adjourning, when the team breaks up. A planned conclusion usually includes recognition for participation and achievement and an opportunity for members to say personal goodbyes. Disbanding a team can create some apprehension, and not all team members handle this well. The termination of the team is a regressive movement from giving up control to the team to giving up inclusion in the team. This last stage focuses on wrapping up activities rather than on task performance.

Strategies for Managing Team Conflict

Conflict isn't always negative; conflict is inevitable, natural, and even healthy whenever people work together. Conflict can be an effective means for everyone to grow, learn, and become more productive and satisfied in the workplace.

What is unhealthy, however, is unresolved conflict that is allowed to fester and become a hindrance to an otherwise productive team. Common causes of conflict include employee competition; differences in objectives, values, or perceptions; disagreements about roles, work activities, or individual styles; and breakdowns in communication.

As a result, conflict management is a big part of managing individuals or teams. To manage conflict, a manager must analyze the conflict situation to determine the cause and severity, and then develop a strategy for action. Strategy options include the following:

- **Avoidance**—withdrawing from or ignoring conflict.

- **Smoothing**—playing down differences to ease conflict.

- **Compromise**—giving up something to gain something.

- **Collaboration**—mutual problem solving.

- **Confrontation**—for verbalization of disagreements.

- **Appeal to team objectives**—highlighting the mutual need to reach a higher goal.

- **Third-party intervention**—asking an objective third party to mediate.

Remember that conflict should be looked upon as an opportunity. When conflict is identified early, managers can prevent small issues from escalating into major, long-term wars in the workplace.

Chapter Check-Out

Q&A

1. In order for a group to be considered a team,
    a. at least two people must be involved.
    b. the members must interact regularly and coordinate their work.
    c. the members must share a common objective.
    d. All of the above.

2. Teams designed to complete a specific task in an organization are called
    a. product development teams.
    b. project teams.
    c. quality teams.
    d. process teams.

3. The stage of group development in which the team members come together to resolve conflict, achieve unity, and understand the roles members pay is:

   a. performing.

   b. storming.

   c. forming.

   d. norming.

4. The benefits of teams include all the following except

   a. flexibility.

   b. commitment.

   c. team training costs.

   d. synergy.

5. When a manager chooses to ignore a conflict situation, the manager is choosing which conflict resolution strategy?

   a. Compromise

   b. Collaboration

   c. Appeal to a superordinate objectives

   d. Avoidance

Answers: 1. d **2.** b **3.** d **4.** c **5.** d

Chapter 11

MOTIVATING AND REWARDING EMPLOYEES

Chapter Check-In

❑ Examining approaches to motivation

❑ Understanding the effects of management philosophies on employee motivation

❑ Structuring the work environment to encourage motivation

Organizations need employees who are committed and motivated and who want to do their jobs well. To create this environment, managers must understand some of the concepts underlying human behavior. This chapter delves into what motivation is and explores methods and techniques managers can use to motivate employees.

Defining Motivation

Many people incorrectly view motivation as a personal trait—that is, some people have it, and others don't. But *motivation* is defined as the force that causes an individual to behave in a specific way. Simply put, a highly motivated person works hard at a job; an unmotivated person does not.

Managers often have difficulty motivating employees. But motivation is really an internal process. It's the result of the interaction of a person's needs, his or her ability to make choices about how to meet those needs, and the environment created by management that allows these needs to be met and the choices to be made. Motivation is not something that a manager can "do" to a person.

Motivation Theories That Focus on Needs

Motivation is a complex phenomenon. Several theories attempt to explain how motivation works. In management circles, probably the most popular explanations of motivation are based on the needs of the individual.

The basic needs model, referred to as **content theory** of motivation, highlights the specific factors that motivate an individual. Although these factors are found within an individual, things outside the individual can affect him or her as well.

In short, all people have needs that they want satisfied. Some are *primary needs,* such as those for food, sleep, and water—needs that deal with the physical aspects of behavior and are considered unlearned. These needs are biological in nature and relatively stable. Their influences on behavior are usually obvious and hence easy to identify.

Secondary needs, on the other hand, are psychological, which means that they are learned primarily through experience. These needs vary significantly by culture and by individual. Secondary needs consist of internal states, such as the desire for power, achievement, and love. Identifying and interpreting these needs is more difficult because they are demonstrated in a variety of ways. Secondary needs are responsible for most of the behavior that a supervisor is concerned with and for the rewards a person seeks in an organization.

Several theorists, including Abraham Maslow, Frederick Herzberg, David McClelland, and Clayton Alderfer, have provided theories to help explain needs as a source of motivation.

Abraham Maslow's hierarchy of needs theory

Abraham Maslow defined **need** as a physiological or psychological deficiency that a person feels the compulsion to satisfy. This need can create tensions that can influence a person's work attitudes and behaviors. Maslow formed a theory based on his definition of need that proposes that humans are motivated by multiple needs and that these needs exist in a hierarchical order. His premise is that only an unsatisfied need can influence behavior; a satisfied need is not a motivator.

Maslow's theory is based on the following two principles:

- **Deficit principle:** A satisfied need no longer motivates behavior because people act to satisfy deprived needs.

■ **Progression principle:** The five needs he identified exist in a hierarchy, which means that a need at any level only comes into play after a lower-level need has been satisfied.

In his theory, Maslow identified five levels of human needs. Table 11-1 illustrates these five levels and provides suggestions for satisfying each need.

Table 11-1   Maslow's Hierarchy of Human Needs

Higher Level Needs	To Satisfy, Offer:
Self-actualization needs	Creative and challenging work
	Participation in decision making
	Job flexibility and autonomy
Esteem needs	Responsibility of an important job
	Promotion to higher status job
	Praise and recognition from boss
Lower Level Needs	**To Satisfy, Offer:**
Social needs	Friendly coworkers
	Interaction with customers
	Pleasant supervisor
Safety needs	Safe working conditions
	Job security
	Base compensation and benefits
Physiological needs	Rest and refreshment breaks
	Physical comfort on the job
	Reasonable work hours

Although research has not verified the strict deficit and progression principles of Maslow's theory, his ideas can help managers understand and satisfy the needs of employees.

Herzberg's two-factor theory

Frederick Herzberg offers another framework for understanding the motivational implications of work environments.

In his **two-factor theory,** Herzberg identifies two sets of factors that impact motivation in the workplace:

■ **Hygiene factors** include salary, job security, working conditions, organizational policies, and technical quality of supervision. Although these factors do not motivate employees, they can cause dissatisfaction if they are missing. Something as simple as adding music to the office place or implementing a no-smoking policy can make people less dissatisfied with these aspects of their work. However, these improvements in hygiene factors do not necessarily increase satisfaction.

■ **Satisfiers** or **motivators** include such things as responsibility, achievement, growth opportunities, and feelings of recognition, and are the key to job satisfaction and motivation. For example, managers can find out what people really do in their jobs and make improvements, thus increasing job satisfaction and performance.

Following Herzberg's two-factor theory, managers need to ensure that hygiene factors are adequate and then build satisfiers into jobs.

Alderfer's ERG theory

Clayton Alderfer's **ERG (Existence, Relatedness, Growth) theory** is built upon Maslow's hierarchy of needs theory. To begin his theory, Alderfer collapses Maslow's five levels of needs into three categories.

■ **Existence needs** are desires for physiological and material well-being. (In terms of Maslow's model, existence needs include physiological and safety needs)

■ **Relatedness needs** are desires for satisfying interpersonal relationships. (In terms of Maslow's model, relatedness correspondence to social needs)

■ **Growth needs** are desires for continued psychological growth and development. (In terms of Maslow's model, growth needs include esteem and self-realization needs)

This approach proposes that unsatisfied needs motivate behavior, and that as lower level needs are satisfied, they become less important. Higher level needs, though, become more important as they are satisfied, and if these needs are not met, a person may move down the hierarchy, which Alderfer calls the *frustration-regression principle.* What he means by this term is that an already satisfied lower level need can become reactivated and influence behavior when a higher level need cannot be satisfied. As a result, managers should provide opportunities for workers to capitalize on the importance of higher level needs.

McClelland's acquired needs theory

David McClelland's acquired needs theory recognizes that everyone prioritizes needs differently. He also believes that individuals are not born with these needs, but that they are actually learned through life experiences. McClelland identifies three specific needs:

- **Need for achievement** is the drive to excel.

- **Need for power** is the desire to cause others to behave in a way that they would not have behaved otherwise.

- **Need for affiliation** is the desire for friendly, close interpersonal relationships and conflict avoidance.

McClelland associates each need with a distinct set of work preferences, and managers can help tailor the environment to meet these needs.

High achievers differentiate themselves from others by their desires to do things better. These individuals are strongly motivated by job situations with personal responsibility, feedback, and an intermediate degree of risk. In addition, high achievers often exhibit the following behaviors:

- Seek personal responsibility for finding solutions to problems

- Want rapid feedback on their performances so that they can tell easily whether they are improving or not

- Set moderately challenging goals and perform best when they perceive their probability of success as 50-50

An individual with a high need of power is likely to follow a path of continued promotion over time. Individuals with a high need of power often demonstrate the following behaviors:

- Enjoy being in charge

- Want to influence others

- Prefer to be placed into competitive and status-oriented situations

- Tend to be more concerned with prestige and gaining influence over others than with effective performance

People with the need for affiliation seek companionship, social approval, and satisfying interpersonal relationships. People needing affiliation display the following behaviors:

- Take a special interest in work that provides companionship and social approval

- Strive for friendship

- Prefer cooperative situations rather than competitive ones

- Desire relationships involving a high degree of mutual understanding

- May not make the best managers because their desire for social approval and friendship may complicate managerial decision making

Interestingly enough, a high need to achieve does not necessarily lead to being a good manager, especially in large organizations. People with high achievement needs are usually interested in how well they do personally and not in influencing others to do well. On the other hand, the best managers are high in their needs for power and low in their needs for affiliation.

Motivation Theories That Focus on Behavior

Another set of theories exists as well. **Process theories** explain how workers select behavioral actions to meet their needs and determine their choices. The following theories each offer advice and insight on how people actually make choices to work hard or not work hard based on their individual preferences, the available rewards, and the possible work outcomes.

Equity theory

According to the equity theory, based on the work of J. Stacy Adams, workers compare the reward potential to the effort they must expend. Equity exists when workers perceive that rewards equal efforts (see Figure 11-1).

But employees just don't look at their potential rewards, they look at the rewards of others as well. Inequities occur when people feel that their rewards are inferior to the rewards offered to other persons sharing the same workloads.

Employees who feel they are being treated inequitably may exhibit the following behaviors:

- Put less effort into their jobs

- Ask for better treatment and/or rewards

- Find ways to make their work seem better by comparison
- Transfer or quit their jobs

Figure 11-1 The equity theory.

The equity theory makes a good point: People behave according to their perceptions. What a manager thinks is irrelevant to an employee because the real issue is the way an employee perceives his or her situation. Rewards perceived as equitable should have positive results on job satisfaction and performance; those rewards perceived as inequitable may create job dissatisfaction and cause performance problems.

Every manager needs to ensure that any negative consequences from equity comparisons are avoided, or at least minimized, when rewards are allocated. Informed managers anticipate perceived negative inequities when especially visible rewards, such as pay increases or promotions, are allocated. Instead of letting equity concerns get out of hand, these managers carefully communicate the intended values of rewards being given, clarify the performance appraisals upon which these rewards are based, and suggest appropriate comparison points.

Expectancy theory

Victor Vroom introduced one of the most widely accepted explanations of motivation. Very simply, the **expectancy theory** says that an employee will be motivated to exert a high level of effort when he or she believes that:

1. Effort will lead to a good performance appraisal.
2. A good appraisal will lead to organizational rewards.
3. The organizational rewards will satisfy his or her personal goals.

The key to the expectancy theory is an understanding of an individual's goals and the relationships between effort and performance, between performance and rewards, and finally, between the rewards and individual goal satisfaction. When an employee has a high level of expectancy and the reward is attractive, motivation is usually high.

Therefore, to motivate workers, managers must strengthen workers' perceptions of their efforts as both possible and worthwhile, clarify expectations of performances, tie rewards to performances, and make sure that rewards are desirable.

Reinforcement theory

The reinforcement theory, based on E. L. Thorndike's law of effect, simply looks at the relationship between behavior and its consequences. This theory focuses on modifying an employee's on-the-job behavior through the appropriate use of one of the following four techniques:

- **Positive reinforcement** rewards desirable behavior. Positive reinforcement, such as a pay raise or promotion, is provided as a reward for positive behavior with the intention of increasing the probability that the desired behavior will be repeated.

- **Avoidance** is an attempt to show an employee what the consequences of improper behavior will be. If an employee does not engage in improper behavior, he or she will not experience the consequence.

- **Extinction** is basically ignoring the behavior of a subordinate and not providing either positive or negative reinforcement. Classroom teachers often use this technique when they ignore students who are "acting out" to get attention. This technique should only be used when the supervisor perceives the behavior as temporary, not typical, and not serious.

- **Punishment** (threats, docking pay, suspension) is an attempt to decrease the likelihood of a behavior recurring by applying negative consequences.

The reinforcement theory has the following implications for management:

- Learning what is acceptable to the organization influences motivated behavior.

- Managers who are trying to motivate their employees should be sure to tell individuals what they are doing wrong and be careful not to reward all individuals at the same time.

■ Managers must tell individuals what they can do to receive positive reinforcement.

■ Managers must be sure to administer the reinforcement as closely as possible to the occurrence of the behavior.

■ Managers must recognize that failure to reward can also modify behavior. Employees who believe that they deserve a reward and do not receive it will often become disenchanted with both their manager and company.

Goal-setting theory

The goal-setting theory, introduced in the late 1960s by Edwin Locke, proposed that intentions to work toward a goal are a major source of work motivation. Goals, in essence, tell employees what needs to be done and how much effort should be expanded. In general, the more difficult the goal, the higher the level of performance expected.

Managers can set the goals for their employees, or employees and managers can develop goals together. One advantage of employees participating in goal setting is that they may be more likely to work toward a goal they helped develop.

No matter who sets the goal, however, employees do better when they get feedback on their progress. In addition to feedback, four other factors influence the goals-performance relationship:

■ The employee must be committed to the goal.

■ The employee must believe that he is capable of performing the task.

■ Tasks involved in achieving the goal should be simple, familiar, and independent.

■ The goal-setting theory is culture bound and is popular in North American cultures.

If the goal-setting theory is followed, managers need to work with their employees in determining goal objectives in order to provide targets for motivation. In addition, the goals that are established should be specific rather than general in nature, and managers must provide feedback on performance.

Management Philosophies That Affect Employee Motivation

Management philosophy can set the foundation for a positive work climate and influence a manager's approach to motivation. The way a manager views employees and communicates with employees affects their behavior.

Two popular theories are Douglas McGregor's Theory X and Theory Y, which talk about how managers create self-fulfilling prophecies based on how they treat their employees. (For a complete description of these theories, refer to Chapter 2.)

Another theory by Chris Argyris centers on what he refers to as the *mature worker*. In his book *Personality and Organization,* Argyris contrasts the management practices found in traditional organizations with the needs and capabilities of the mature adult personality.

For example, the concept of work specialization is supposed to make people work more efficiently because the tasks are very defined. Argyris believes that this concept may actually be counterproductive because it will limit an employee from reaching self-actualization.

Like McGregor, Argyris is concerned about how managers treat people. He believes that if managers treat their employees in a positive manner— as responsible adults—their employees will be more productive. However, Argyris takes this concept one step further. He believes that mature workers want additional responsibilities, a variety of tasks, and the ability to participate in decisions. If not, he believes that the result will be employee absenteeism, apathy, and even alienation.

Motivation Strategies

To some extent, a high level of employee motivation is derived from effective management practices. To develop motivated employees, a manager must treat people as individuals, empower workers, provide an effective reward system, redesign jobs, and create a flexible workplace.

Empowering employees

Empowerment occurs when individuals in an organization are given autonomy, authority, trust, and encouragement to accomplish a task. Empowerment is designed to unshackle the worker and to make a job the worker's responsibility.

In an attempt to empower and to change some of the old bureaucratic ideas, managers are promoting corporate intrapreneurships. **Intrapreneurship** encourages employees to pursue new ideas and gives them the authority to promote those ideas. Obviously, intrapreneurship is not for the timid, because old structures and processes are turned upside down.

Providing an effective reward system

Managers often use rewards to reinforce employee behavior that they want to continue. A *reward* is a work outcome of positive value to the individual. Organizations are rich in rewards for people whose performance accomplishments help meet organizational objectives. People receive rewards in one of the following two ways:

- **Extrinsic rewards** are externally administered. They are valued outcomes given to someone by another person, typically a supervisor or higher level manager. Common workplace examples are pay bonuses, promotions, time off, special assignments, office fixtures, awards, verbal praise, and so on. In all cases, the motivational stimulus of extrinsic rewards originates outside the individual.

- **Intrinsic rewards** are self-administered. Think of the "natural high" a person may experience after completing a job. That person feels good because she has a feeling of competency, personal development, and self-control over her work. In contrast to extrinsic rewards, the motivational stimulus of intrinsic rewards is internal and doesn't depend on the actions of other people.

To motivate behavior, the organization needs to provide an effective reward system. An effective reward system has four elements:

- Rewards need to satisfy the basic needs of all employees.

- Rewards need to be included in the system and be comparable to ones offered by a competitive organization in the same area.

- Rewards need to be available to people in the same positions and be distributed fairly and equitably.

- The overall reward system needs to be multifaceted. Because all people are different, managers must provide a range of rewards—pay, time off, recognition, or promotion. In addition, managers should provide several different ways to earn these rewards.

This last point is worth noting. With the widely developing trend toward empowerment in American industry, many employees and employers are beginning to view traditional pay systems as inadequate. In a traditional system, people are paid according to the positions they hold, not the contributions they make. As organizations adopt approaches built upon teams, customer satisfaction, and empowerment, workers need to be paid differently. Many companies have already responded by designing numerous pay plans, designed by employee design teams, which base rewards on skill levels.

Rewards demonstrate to employees that their behavior is appropriate and should be repeated. If employees don't feel that their work is valued, their motivation will decline.

Redesigning jobs

Many people go to work every day and go through the same, unenthusiastic actions to perform their jobs. These individuals often refer to this condition as burnout. But smart managers can do something to improve this condition before an employee becomes bored and loses motivation. The concept of *job redesign,* which requires a knowledge of and concern for the human qualities people bring with them to the organization, applies motivational theories to the structure of work for improving productivity and satisfaction

When redesigning jobs, managers look at both job scope and job depth. Redesign attempts may include the following:

- **Job enlargement.** Often referred to as *horizontal job loading,* job enlargement increases the variety of tasks a job includes. Although it doesn't increase the quality or the challenge of those tasks, job enlargement may reduce some of the monotony, and as an employee's boredom decreases, his or her work quality generally increases.

- **Job rotation.** This practice assigns people to different jobs or tasks to different people on a temporary basis. The idea is to add variety and to expose people to the dependence that one job has on other jobs. Job rotation can encourage higher levels of contributions and renew interest and enthusiasm. The organization benefits from a cross-trained workforce.

- **Job enrichment.** Also called *vertical job loading,* this application includes not only an increased variety of tasks, but also provides an employee with more responsibility and authority. If the skills required to do the job are skills that match the jobholder's abilities, job enrichment may improve morale and performance.

Creating flexibility

Today's employees value personal time. Because of family needs, a traditional nine-to-five workday may not work for many people. Therefore, **flextime,** which permits employees to set and control their own work hours, is one way that organizations are accommodating their employees' needs. Here are some other options organizations are trying as well:

- A **compressed workweek** is a form of flextime that allows a full-time job to be completed in less than the standard 40-hour, five-day workweek. Its most common form is the 4/40 schedule, which gives employees three days off each week. This schedule benefits the individual through more leisure time and lower commuting costs. The organization should benefit through lower absenteeism and improved performance. Of course, the danger in this type of scheduling is the possibility of increased fatigue.

- **Job sharing** or **twinning** occurs when one full-time job is split between two or more persons. Job sharing often involves each person working one-half day, but it can also be done on weekly or monthly sharing arrangements. When jobs can be split and shared, organizations can benefit by employing talented people who would otherwise be unable to work full-time. The qualified employee who is also a parent may not want to be in the office for a full day but may be willing to work a half-day. Although adjustment problems sometimes occur, the arrangement can be good for all concerned.

- **Telecommuting,** sometimes called *flexiplace,* is a work arrangement that allows at least a portion of scheduled work hours to be completed outside of the office, with work-at-home as one of the options. Telecommuting frees the jobholder from needing to work fixed hours, wearing special work attire, enduring the normal constraints of commuting, and having direct contact with supervisors. Home workers often demonstrate increased productivity, report fewer distractions, enjoy the freedom to be their own boss, and appreciate the benefit of having more time for themselves.

Of course, when there are positives, there are also negatives. Many home workers feel that they work too much and are isolated from their family and friends. In addition to the feelings of isolation, many employees feel that the lack of visibility at the office may result in the loss of promotions.

Chapter Checkout

Q&A

1. Motivational theories that emphasize the needs that motivate people are called

   a. process theories.
   b. goal-setting theories.
   c. content theories.
   d. path-goal theories.

2. All of the following are examples of hygiene factors except

   a. the work itself.
   b. salary.
   c. company policies.
   d. working conditions.

3. According to Alderfer's ERG theory, existence needs can be described as

   a. needs for satisfactory relationships with others.
   b. calls for realizations of potential.
   c. calls for the achievements of competence.
   d. a person's well being.

4. According to expectancy theory, the intensity of motivation functions is

   a. very difficult to determine.
   b. indirectly proportional to perceived rewards.
   c. directly proportional to perceived or expected rewards.
   d. indirectly proportional to expected rewards.

5. When a manager redesigns a job so that the job includes an increased number of tasks, but does not address the issues of the quality of the challenge of the tasks, the manager is utilizing

   a. job depth.
   b. job rotation.
   c. job enrichment.
   d. job enlargement.

Answers: 1. c **2.** a **3.** d **4.** c **5.** d

Chapter 12

LEADERSHIP AND MANAGEMENT

Chapter Check-In

❑ Defining leadership traits and skills

❑ Identifying leadership styles

❑ Examining approaches to leadership

❑ Understanding challenges facing today's leaders

Traditionally, the term management refers to the activities (and often the group of people) involved in five general functions: planning, organizing, staffing, leading, and controlling. Managers perform and integrate these five functions, discussed in Chapter 1, throughout their organizations. However, emerging trends in management point out that leading people is different than managing them.

Many people believe that leadership is simply being the first, biggest, or most powerful person. But leadership in organizations has a different and more meaningful definition. This chapter looks at the definition of leadership, as well as its major theories and styles. Traits and characteristics that leaders should demonstrate are also addressed.

Leadership Defined

Leading is establishing direction and influencing others to follow that direction. But this definition isn't as simple as it sounds because leadership has many variations and different areas of emphasis.

Common to all definitions of leadership is the notion that leaders are individuals who, by their actions, facilitate the movement of a group of people toward a common or shared goal. This definition implies that leadership is an influence process.

The distinction between leader and leadership is important, but potentially confusing. The leader is an individual; leadership is the function or activity this individual performs. The word leader is often used interchangeably with the word manager to describe those individuals in an organization who have positions of formal authority, regardless of how they actually act in those jobs. But just because a manager is supposed to be a formal leader in an organization doesn't mean that he or she exercises leadership.

An issue often debated among business professionals is whether leadership is a different function and activity from management. Harvard's John Kotter says that management is about coping with complexity, and leadership, in contrast, is about coping with change. He also states that leadership is an important part of management, but only a part; management also requires planning, organizing, staffing, and controlling. Management produces a degree of predictability and order. Leadership produces change. Kotter believes that most organizations are underled and overmanaged. He sees both strong leadership and strong management as necessary for optimal organizational effectiveness.

Leadership traits

Theories abound to explain what makes an effective leader. The oldest theories attempt to identify the common traits or skills that make an effective leader. Contemporary theorists and theories concentrate on actions of leaders rather than characteristics.

A number of traits that appear regularly in leaders include ambition, energy, the desire to lead, self-confidence, and intelligence. Although certain traits are helpful, these attributes provide no guarantees that a person possessing them is an effective leader. Underlying the trait approach is the assumption that some people are natural leaders, and are endowed with certain traits not possessed by other individuals. This research compared successful and unsuccessful leaders to see how they differed in physical characteristics, personality, and ability.

A recent published analysis of leadership traits (S.A. Kirkpatrick and E.A. Locke, *"Leadership: Do Traits Really Matter?"* Academy of Management Executive 5 [1991]) identified six core characteristics that the majority of effective leaders possess:

- **Drive.** Leaders are ambitious and take initiative.
- **Motivation.** Leaders want to lead and are willing to take charge.

- **Honesty and integrity.** Leaders are truthful and do what they say they will do.

- **Self-confidence.** Leaders are assertive and decisive and enjoy taking risks. They admit mistakes and foster trust and commitment to a vision. Leaders are emotionally stable rather than recklessly adventurous.

- **Cognitive ability.** Leaders are intelligent, perceptive, and conceptually skilled, but are not necessarily geniuses. They show analytical ability, good judgment, and the capacity to think strategically.

- **Business knowledge.** Leaders tend to have technical expertise in their businesses.

Traits do a better job at predicting that a manger may be an effective leader rather than actually distinguishing between an effective or ineffective leader. Because workplace situations vary, leadership requirements vary. As a result, researchers began to examine what effective leaders do rather than what effective leaders are. Leadership styles and behaviors are addressed in the next section.

Leadership skills

Whereas traits are the characteristics of leaders, skills are the knowledge and abilities, or *competencies,* of leaders. The competencies a leader needs depends upon the situation:

These competencies depend on a variety of factors:

- The number of people following the leader

- The extent of the leader's leadership skills

- The leader's basic nature and values

- The group or organization's background, such as whether it's for profit or not-for-profit, new or long established, large or small

- The particular culture (or values and associated behaviors) of whomever is being led

To help managers refine these skills, leadership-training programs typically propose guidelines for making decisions, solving problems, exercising power and influence, and building trust.

Peter Drucker, one of the best-known contemporary management theorists, offers a pragmatic approach to leadership in the workplace. He believes that consistency is the key to good leadership, and that successful leaders share the following three abilities which are based on what he refers to as good old-fashioned hard work:

- **To define and establish a sense of mission.** Good leaders set goals, priorities, and standards, making sure that these objectives not only are communicated but maintained.

- **To accept leadership as a responsibility rather than a rank.** Good leaders aren't afraid to surround themselves with talented, capable people; they do not blame others when things go wrong.

- **To earn and keep the trust of others.** Good leaders have personal integrity and inspire trust among their followers; their actions are consistent with what they say.

In Drucker's words, "Effective leadership is not based on being clever, it is based primarily on being consistent."

Very simply put, leading is establishing direction and influencing others to follow that direction. Keep in mind that no list of leadership traits and skills is definitive because no two successful leaders are alike. What is important is that leaders exhibit some positive characteristics that make them effective managers at any level in an organization.

Leadership styles

No matter what their traits or skills, leaders carry out their roles in a wide variety of styles. Some leaders are autocratic. Others are democratic. Some are participatory, and others are hands off. Often, the leadership style depends on the situation, including where the organization is in its life cycle. (Chapter 7 talks about the life cycles of organizations).

The following are common leadership styles:

- **Autocratic.** The manager makes all the decisions and dominates team members. This approach generally results in passive resistance from team members and requires continual pressure and direction from the leader in order to get things done. Generally, this approach is not a good way to get the best performance from a team. However, this style may be appropriate when urgent action is necessary or when subordinates actually prefer this style.

- **Participative.** The manager involves the subordinates in decision making by consulting team members (while still maintaining control), which encourages employee ownership for the decisions.

A good participative leader encourages participation and delegates wisely, but never loses sight of the fact that he or she bears the crucial responsibility of leadership. The leader values group discussions and input from team members; he or she maximizes the members' strong points in order to obtain the best performance from the entire team. The participative leader motivates team members by empowering them to direct themselves; he or she guides them with a loose rein. The downside, however, is that a participative leader may be seen as unsure, and team members may feel that everything is a matter for group discussion and decision.

- **Laissez-faire** (also called free-rein). In this hands-off approach, the leader encourages team members to function independently and work out their problems by themselves, although he or she is available for advice and assistance. The leader usually has little control over team members, leaving them to sort out their roles and tackle their work assignments without personally participating in these processes. In general, this approach leaves the team floundering with little direction or motivation. Laissez-faire is usually only appropriate when the team is highly motivated and skilled, and has a history of producing excellent work.

Many experts believe that overall leadership style depends largely on a manager's beliefs, values, and assumptions. How managers approach the following three elements—motivation, decision making, and task orientation—affect their leadership styles:

- **Motivation.** Leaders influence others to reach goals through their approaches to motivation. They can use either positive or negative motivation. A positive style uses praise, recognition, and rewards, and increases employee security and responsibility. A negative style uses punishment, penalties, potential job loss, suspension, threats, and reprimands.

- **Decision making.** The second element of a manager's leadership style is the degree of decision authority the manager grants employees—ranging from no involvement to group decision making.

- **Task** and **employee orientation.** The final element of leadership style is the manager's perspective on the most effective way to get the work done. Managers who favor task orientation emphasize getting work done by using better methods or equipment, controlling the work environment, assigning and organizing work, and monitoring performance. Managers who favor employee orientation emphasize getting work done through meeting the human needs of subordinates. Teamwork, positive relationships, trust, and problem solving are the major focuses of the employee-oriented manager.

Keep in mind that managers may exhibit both task and employee orientations to some degree.

The managerial grid model, shown in Figure 12-1 and developed by Robert Blake and Jane Mouton, identifies five leadership styles with varying concerns for people and production:

Figure 12-1 Blake-Mouton Managerial Grid.

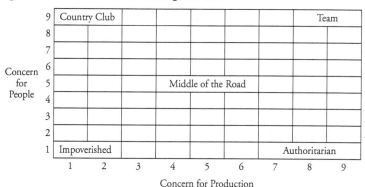

- The **impoverished style,** located at the lower left-hand corner of the grid, point (1, 1), is characterized by low concern for both people and production; its primary objective is for managers to stay out of trouble.

- The **country club style,** located at the upper left-hand corner of the grid, point (1, 9), is distinguished by high concern for people and a low concern for production; its primary objective is to create a secure and comfortable atmosphere where managers trust that subordinates will respond positively.

- The **authoritarian style,** located at the lower right-hand corner of the grid, point (9,1), is identified by high concern for production and low concern for people; its primary objective is to achieve the organization's goals, and employee needs are not relevant in this process.

- The **middle-of-the-road style,** located at the middle of the grid, point (5, 5), maintains a balance between workers' needs and the organization's productivity goals; its primary objective is to maintain employee morale at a level sufficient to get the organization's work done.

■ The **team style,** located at the upper right-hand of the grid, point (9, 9), is characterized by high concern for people and production; its primary objective is to establish cohesion and foster a feeling of commitment among workers.

The Managerial Grid model suggests that competent leaders should use a style that reflects the highest concern for both people and production—point (9.9), team-oriented style.

Power versus authority

Effective leaders develop and use power, or the ability to influence others. The traditional manager's power comes from his or her position within the organization. Legitimate, reward, and coercive are all forms of power used by managers to change employee behavior and are defined as follows:

■ **Legitimate power** stems from a formal management position in an organization and the authority granted to it. Subordinates accept this as a legitimate source of power and comply with it.

■ **Reward power** stems from the authority to reward others. Managers can give formal rewards, such as pay increases or promotions, and may also use praise, attention, and recognition to influence behavior.

■ **Coercive power** is the opposite of reward power and stems from the authority to punish or to recommend punishment. Managers have coercive power when they have the right to fire or demote employees, criticize them, withhold pay increases, give reprimands, make negative entries in employee files, and so on.

Keep in mind that different types of position power receive different responses in followers. Legitimate power and reward power are most likely to generate compliance, where workers obey orders even though they may personally disagree with them. Coercive power most often generates resistance, which may lead workers to deliberately avoid carrying out instructions or to disobey orders.

Unlike external sources of position power, personal power most often comes from internal sources, such as a person's special knowledge or personality characteristics. Personal power is the tool of a leader. Subordinates follow a leader because of respect, admiration, or caring they feel for this individual and his or her ideas. The following two types of personal power exist:

■ **Expert power** results from a leader's special knowledge or skills regarding the tasks performed by followers. When a leader is a true expert, subordinates tend to go along quickly with his or her recommendations.

■ **Referent power** results from leadership characteristics that command identification, respect, and admiration from subordinates who then desire to emulate the leader. When workers admire a supervisor because of the way he or she deals with them, the influence is based on referent power. Referent power depends on a leader's personal characteristics rather than on his or her formal title or position, and is most visible in the area of charismatic leadership.

The most common follower response to expert power and referent power is commitment. Commitment means that workers share the leader's point of view and enthusiastically carry out instructions. Needless to say, commitment is preferred to compliance or resistance. Commitment helps followers overcome fear of change, and it is especially important in those instances.

Keep in mind that the different types of power described in this section are interrelated. Most leaders use a combination of these types of power, depending on the leadership style used. Authoritarian leaders, for example, use a mixture of legitimate, coercive and reward powers to dictate the policies, plans, and activities of a group. In comparison, a participative leader uses mainly referent power, involving all members of the group in the decision-making process.

Situational Approaches to Leadership

The theme in early approaches to understanding leadership was the desire to identify traits or behaviors that effective leaders had in common. A common set of characteristics proved to be elusive, however. Researchers were continually frustrated by the lack of consistent support for their findings and conclusions. As a result, research began to focus on what style of leadership was most effective in a particular situation. **Contingency** or **situational theories** examine the fit between the leader and the situation and provide guidelines for managers to achieve this effective fit.

The theorists in this section believe that managers choose leadership styles based on leadership situations. Managers adjust their decision-making, orientation, and motivational approaches based upon a unique combination of factors in their situations: characteristics of employees, types of work, organizational structures, personal preferences, and upper-level management's influences.

The following sections describe the three most well-known situational theories.

Fiedler's contingency theory

Fred E. Fiedler's contingency theory centers on the belief that there is no best way for managers to lead. Different situations create different leadership style requirements for managers. The style that works in one environment may not work in another.

Fiedler looked at three elements that dictate a leader's situational control. These elements are:

- **Task structure.** Is the job highly structured, fairly unstructured, or somewhere in between? The spelling out in detail (favorable) of what is required of subordinates affects task structure.

- **Leader/member relations.** This element applies to the amount of loyalty, dependability, and support that a leader receives from his or her employees. In a favorable relationship, a manager has a highly formed task structure and is able to reward and/or punish employees without any problems. In an unfavorable relationship, the task structure is usually poorly formed, and the leader possesses limited authority.

- **Positioning power.** Positioning power measures the amount of power or authority a manager perceives the organization has given him or her for the purpose of directing, rewarding, and punishing subordinates. Positioning powers of managers depends on the taking away (favorable) or increasing (unfavorable) of the decision-making power of employees.

Fiedler then rated managers as to whether they were relationship oriented or task oriented. Task-oriented managers tended to do better in situations with good leader/member relationships, structured tasks, and either weak or strong position power. They also did well when the tasks were unstructured, but position power was strong, as well as when the leader/member relations were moderate to poor and the tasks were unstructured. Relationship-oriented managers, on the other hand, do better in all other situations.

The task-motivated style leader experiences pride and satisfaction in task accomplishment for his or her organization, while the relationship-motivated style leader seeks to build interpersonal relations and extend extra help for team development in his or her organization.

Judging whether a leadership style is good or bad can be difficult. Each manager has his or her own preferences for leadership. Task-motivated leaders are at their best when their teams perform successfully—such as achieving new sales records or outperforming major competitors. Relationship-oriented leaders are at their best when greater customer satisfaction is gained and positive company images are established.

Hersey-Blanchard's situational model

The Hersey-Blanchard Model of Situational Leadership, shown in Figure 12-2, is based on the amount of direction (task behavior) and amount of socioemotional support (relationship behavior) a leader must provide given the situation and the level of maturity of the followers.

Figure 12-2 Hersey-Blanchard's Model of Situational Leadership.

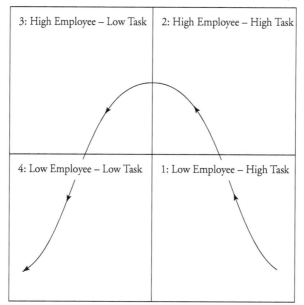

Task behavior is the extent to which the leader engages in spelling out the duties and responsibilities to an individual or group. This behavior includes telling people what to do, how to do it, when to do it, and where to do it.

In task behavior, the leader engages in one-way communication. *Relationship behavior,* on the other hand, is the extent to which the leader engages in two-way or multiway communications. This behavior includes listening to, facilitating, and supporting employees. And *maturity* is the willingness and ability of a person to take responsibility for directing his own behavior. Employees tend to have varying degrees of maturity, depending on the specific tasks, functions, or objectives that they attempt to accomplish.

To determine the appropriate leadership style to use in a given situation, a leader must first determine the maturity levels of his or her followers in relationship to the specific task. As employee maturity levels increase, a leader should begin to reduce task behavior and increase relationship behavior until his or her followers reach moderate maturity levels. As the employees move into above-average maturity levels, the leader should decrease not only task behavior but also relationship behavior.

Once maturity levels are identified, a manager can determine the appropriate leadership style: telling, selling, participating, or delegating.

- **Telling.** This style reflects high task/low relationship behavior (S1). The leader provides clear instructions and specific direction. Telling style is best matched with a low follower readiness level.

- **Selling.** This style reflects high task/high relationship behavior (S2). The leader encourages two-way communication and helps build confidence and motivation on the part of the employee, although the leader still has responsibility and controls decision making. Selling style is best matched with a moderate follower readiness level.

- **Participating.** This style reflects high relationship/low task behavior (S3). With this style, the leader and followers share decision making and no longer need or expect the relationship to be directive. Participating style is best matched with a moderate follower readiness level.

- **Delegating.** This style reflects low relationship/low task behavior (S4). Delegating style is appropriate for leaders whose followers are ready to accomplish a particular task and are both competent and motivated to take full responsibility. This style is best matched with a high follower readiness level.

House's path-goal theory

The path-goal theory, developed by Robert House, is based on the expectancy theory of motivation (see Chapter 11). A manager's job is to coach or guide workers to choose the best paths for reaching their goals. Based on the goal-setting theory, leaders engage in different types of leadership behaviors depending on the nature and demands of a particular situation.

A leader's behavior is acceptable to subordinates when viewed as a source of satisfaction. He or she is motivational when need satisfaction is contingent on performance, and this leader facilitates, coaches, and rewards effective performance. Path-goal theory identifies several leadership styles:

- **Achievement-oriented.** The leader sets challenging goals for followers, expects them to perform at their highest levels, and shows confidence in their abilities to meet these expectations. This style is appropriate when followers lack job challenges.

- **Directive.** The leader lets followers know what is expected of them and tells them how to perform their tasks. This style is appropriate when followers hold ambiguous jobs.

- **Participative.** The leader consults with followers and asks them for suggestions before making a decision. This style is appropriate when followers are using improper procedures or are making poor decisions.

- **Supportive.** The leader is friendly and approachable. He or she shows concern for the followers' psychological well-being. This style is appropriate when followers lack confidence.

Path-goal theory assumes that leaders are flexible and that they can change their styles as situations require. This theory proposes two contingency variables that moderate the leader behavior-outcome relationship:

- **Environment** characteristics are outside the control of followers, task structure, authority system, and work group. Environmental factors determine the type of leader behavior required if follower outcomes are to be maximized.

- **Follower** characteristics are the focus of control, experience, and perceived ability. Personal characteristics of subordinates determine how the environment and leader behavior are interpreted.

Effective leaders clarify the path to help their followers achieve their goals, and make their journeys easier by reducing roadblocks and pitfalls. Research demonstrates that employee performance and satisfaction are positively influenced when leaders compensate for shortcomings in either their employees or the work settings.

Challenges Facing Leaders

Organizations today place multiple demands on leaders, requiring them to impart vision, initiate change, and make difficult decisions. To handle these demands, leaders must be flexible and adaptable.

Transformational leadership

Transformational leadership blends the behavioral theories with a little dab of trait theories. Transactional leaders, such as those identified in contingency theories, guide followers in the direction of established goals by clarifying role and task requirements. However, transformational leaders, who are charismatic and visionary, can inspire followers to transcend their own self-interest for the good of their organizations.

Transformational leaders appeal to followers' ideals and moral values and inspire them to think about problems in new or different ways. These leaders influence followers through vision, framing, and impression management.

Vision is the ability of the leader to bind people together with an idea. Framing is the process whereby leaders define the purpose of their movements in highly meaningful terms. Impression management is an attempt to control the impressions that others form of a leader by practicing behaviors that make him or her more attractive and appealing to others.

A transformational leader instills feelings of confidence, admiration, and commitment in his or her followers. This type of leader is charismatic, creating a special bond with followers, articulating a vision with which his or her followers identify and for which these followers are willing to work. Each follower is coached, advised, and delegated some authority. The transformational leader stimulates followers intellectually, arousing them to develop new ways to think about problems. This leader uses contingent rewards to positively reinforce performances that are consistent with his or her wishes. Management is by exception. Transformational leaders take initiative only when problems occur and are not actively involved when things are going well. He or she commits people to actions and converts followers into leaders.

Research indicates that transformational, as compared to transactional, leadership is more strongly correlated with lower turnover rates, higher productivity, and higher employee satisfaction.

Transformational leaders are relevant to today's workplace because they are flexible and innovative. Although it is important to have leaders with the appropriate orientation defining tasks and managing interrelationships, it is even more important to have leaders who can bring organizations into futures they have not yet imagined. Transformational leadership is the essence of creating and sustaining competitive advantage.

Change leadership

Today's business world is highly competitive. The way for an organization to survive is by reshaping to meet the needs of a rapidly changing world. Resistance to change is a dead-end street for employees and for the organization. Leaders need to emphasize action to make the change as quickly and smoothly as possible.

As discussed in Chapter 7, organizations go through a four-stage life cycle. For some organizations, the four periods of growth come and go very rapidly; for others, that process may take decades. Failure to follow through with the needed changes in any of the four growth periods could mean the end for an organization.

Throughout these periods of change, which is just about all the time for a good organization, leaders must concentrate on having their people go from change avoidance to change acceptance. The five steps that accompany change—for individuals facing life-altering circumstances and for organizations facing fundamental shifts—are denial, anger, bargaining, depression, and finally, acceptance.

Often a worker's first reaction to change is to resist it. An employee becomes comfortable performing tasks and processes a certain way. These comfort levels provide employees with the security of knowing that they are the masters of their work environment. Employees fear that change could disrupt their lives by making their jobs harder or causing them to lose their sense of control.

Leaders can help the change process by changing their employees' attitudes from avoidance into acceptance. This change is accomplished by managers as strong leaders transforming their employees' avoidance questions and statements into acceptance questions:

- **From "Why?" to "What new opportunities will this change provide?"** When employees ask "why," a manager should focus on the benefits that the change will provide employees and the organization.

- **From "How will this affect me?" to "What problems will this solve?"** Managers should let employees know what the problem is and how they will be part of the solution.

- **From "We do not do it this way" to "What will be the result if we do it this new way?"** One of the first reactions is that a process never has been done this way. Managers should provide explanations and empathy.

- **From "When will this be over so that we can get back to work?" to "What can I do to help?"** Managers should get employees involved in implementing the change.

Managers need to keep in mind that feelings are contagious. By positively promoting a change, a leader makes others want to be part of it. Managers should also give employees the necessary authority and control to help bring the change about. So that employees do not feel powerless, managers should share their responsibilities. A manager should want his or her team members to feel useful and enthusiastic. Employees should be made to feel as if the change could not have happened without them.

Leading in the learning organization

An organization that encourages learning among its people is referred to as a **learning organization.** In a learning organization, employees are engaged in identifying and solving problems, enabling the organization to continuously experiment, change, and improve. Thus, the organization can increase its capacity to grow, learn, and achieve its purpose.

In the learning organization, all employees look for problems, such as understanding special customer needs. Employees also solve problems, which means putting things together in unique ways to meet customer needs. A learning organization promotes exchanges of information among employees, which creates a more knowledgeable workforce. Learning organizations exhibit flexibility because employees accept and adapt to new ideas and changes through a shared vision.

Today's increased pace of change is one reason the learning organization is popular. The corporation that is able to quickly shape and motivate their workers is better able to transform its work practices to keep pace with the constantly changing environment.

Leadership in learning organizations requires something more than the traditional approach of setting goals, making decisions, and directing the troops. In learning organizations, managers learn to think in terms of "control with" rather than "control over" employees. They "control with" employees by building relationships based on shared visions and shaping the cultures of their organizations so that all can help achieve the same visions. A leader in this learning environment can help facilitate teamwork, initiate change, and expand the capacity of employees to shape their organization's future. Leaders who understand how the learning organization operates can help other leaders adapt to this organizational style.

Visionary leadership, a team-based structure, participative strategy, a strong, adaptive internal culture, empowered employees, and open information characterize the learning organization. Consultant Peter Senge, author of the popular book, *The Fifth Discipline,* identifies the following ingredients of learning organizations:

- **Mental models**—setting aside of old ways of thinking

- **Personal mastery**—self-awareness and ability to remain open to others

- **Systems thinking**—understanding of the plan of action

- **Shared vision**—mutual agreement to the plan of action

- **Team learning**—working together to accomplish the plan of action

Senge's concept of the learning organization places high value on developing the ability to learn and then make that learning continuously available to all organizational members.

Chapter Checkout

Q&A

1. Several studies regarding leadership traits have proven which of the following:
   a. Leadership traits are universal.
   b. No specific list of successful leadership traits exists.
   c. Leadership traits, skills, and behaviors are common.
   d. Successful leaders have similar personalities.

2. Which type of power is least associated with the autocratic style of leadership?
   a. Referent
   b. Expert
   c. Formal
   d. Nonconforming

3. When sport coaches listen to players' suggestions and feedback during game intermission, they are using what type of leadership?

   a. Free-rein

   b. Autocratic

   c. General

   d. Participating

4. The contingency, path-goal, and life-cycle theories of leadership are considered

   a. autocratic.

   b. organizational.

   c. situational.

   d. unrealistic.

5. Vision, charisma, integrity, and symbolism are all on the list of attributes associated with what type of leaders?

   a. Contingency

   b. Informal

   c. Transformational

   d. Transactional

Answers: 1. b **2.** a **3.** d **4.** c **5.** c

Chapter 13

COMMUNICATION AND
INTERPERSONAL SKILLS

Chapter Check-In

❑   Understanding the importance of communication in business

❑   Communicating as a process

❑   Differentiating between interpersonal and organizational communication methods

❑   Promoting effective communication

No function is more vital to management than communication. Communication is at the heart of every business activity; it is the thread that ties the actions of the individual or organization to its desired objectives. Communication is the way that employees share feelings, thoughts, wants, and needs.

Communication doesn't always come naturally, though. Although the communication skills of human beings are much more developed than those of any other organisms, most people are still relatively poor transmitters of ideas. And surprisingly enough, many studies indicate the employees and managers identify lack of communication as the most common problem in their organizations.

In this chapter, the guidelines for successful communication, including oral, written, verbal, interpersonal, and organizational are presented.

The Significance of Communication in the Management Process

Organizations are totally reliant on **communication,** which is defined as the exchange of ideas, messages, or information by speech, signals, or writing. Without communication, organizations would not function. If communication is diminished or hampered, the entire organization suffers. When communication is thorough, accurate, and timely, the organization tends to be vibrant and effective.

Communication is central to the entire management process for four primary reasons:

- **Communication is a linking process of management.** Communication is the way managers conduct the managerial functions of planning, organizing, staffing, directing, and controlling. Communication is the heart of all organizations

- **Communication is the primary means by which people obtain and exchange information.** Decisions are often dependent upon the quality and quantity of the information received. If the information on which a decision is based is poor or incomplete, the decision will often be incorrect.

- **The most time-consuming activity a manager engages in is communication.** Managers spend between 70 to 90 percent of their time communicating with employees and other internal and external customers.

- **Information and communication represent power in organizations.** An employee cannot do anything constructive in a work unit unless he or she knows what is to be done, when the task is to be accomplished, and who else is involved. The staff members who have this information become centers of power.

The ability to communicate well, both orally and in writing, is a critical managerial skill and a foundation of effective leadership. Through communication, people exchange and share information with one another and influence one another's attitudes, behaviors, and understandings. Communication allows managers to establish and maintain interpersonal relationships, listen to others, and otherwise gain the information needed to create an inspirational workplace. No manager can handle conflict, negotiate successfully, and succeed at leadership without being a good communicator.

The Communication Process

The goal of communication is to convey information—and the understanding of that information—from one person or group to another person or group. This communication process is divided into three basic components: A *sender* transmits a message through a *channel* to the *receiver.* (Figure 13-1 shows a more elaborate model.) The sender first develops an idea, which is composed into a message and then transmitted to the other party, who interprets the message and receives meaning. Information theorists have added somewhat more complicated language. Developing a message is known as *encoding.* Interpreting the message is referred to as *decoding.*

Figure 13-1 Communication model.

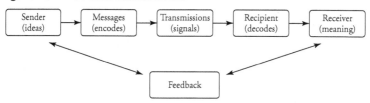

The other important feature is the feedback cycle. When two people interact, communication is rarely one-way only. When a person receives a message, she responds to it by giving a reply. The feedback cycle is the same as the sender-receiver feedback noted in Figure 13-1. Otherwise, the sender can't know whether the other parties properly interpreted the message or how they reacted to it. Feedback is especially significant in management because a supervisor has to know how subordinates respond to directives and plans. The manager also needs to know how work is progressing and how employees feel about the general work situation.

The critical factor in measuring the effectiveness of communication is common understanding. Understanding exists when all parties involved have a mutual agreement as to not only the information, but also the meaning of the information. Effective communication, therefore, occurs when the intended message of the sender and the interpreted message of the receiver are one and the same. Although this should be the goal in any communication, it is not always achieved.

The most efficient communication occurs at a minimum cost in terms of resources expended. Time, in particular, is an important resource in the communication process. For example, it would be virtually impossible for an instructor to take the time to communicate individually with each student in a class about every specific topic covered. Even if it were possible, it would be costly. This is why managers often leave voice mail messages and interact by e-mail rather than visit their subordinates personally.

However, efficient time-saving communications are not always effective. A low-cost approach such as an e-mail note to a distribution list may save time, but it does not always result in everyone getting the same meaning from the message. Without opportunities to ask questions and clarify the message, erroneous interpretations are possible. In addition to a poor choice of communication method, other barriers to effective communication include noise and other physical distractions, language problems, and failure to recognize nonverbal signals.

Sometimes communication is effective, but not efficient. A work team leader visiting each team member individually to explain a new change in procedures may guarantee that everyone truly understands the change, but this method may be very costly on the leader's time. A team meeting would be more efficient. In these and other ways, potential tradeoffs between effectiveness and efficiency occur.

Methods of Communication

The standard methods of communication are speaking or writing by a sender and listening or reading by the receiver. Most communication is oral, with one party speaking and others listening.

However, some forms of communication do not directly involve spoken or written language. **Nonverbal communication** (body language) consists of actions, gestures, and other aspects of physical appearance that, combined with facial expressions (such as smiling or frowning), can be powerful means of transmitting messages. At times, a person's body may be "talking" even as he or she maintains silence. And when people do speak, their bodies may sometimes say different things than their words convey. A *mixed message* occurs when a person's words communicate one message, while nonverbally, he or she is communicating something else.

Although technology such as e-mail has lessened the importance of nonverbal communication, the majority of organizational communication still takes place through face-to-face interaction. Every verbal message comes with a nonverbal component. Receivers interpret messages by taking in meaning from everything available. When nonverbal cues are consistent with verbal messages, they act to reinforce the messages. But when these verbal and nonverbal messages are inconsistent, they create confusion for the receiver.

The actions of management are especially significant because subordinates place more confidence in what managers do than what they say. Unless actions are consistent with communication, a feeling of distrust will undermine the effectiveness of any future social exchange.

Oral communication skills

Because a large part of a manager's day is spent conversing with other managers and employees, the abilities to speak and listen are critical to success. For example, oral communication skills are used when a manager must make sales presentations, conduct interviews, perform employee evaluations, and hold press conferences.

In general, managers prefer to rely on oral communication because communication tends to be more complete and thorough when talking in person. In face-to-face interactions, a person can judge how the other party is reacting, get immediate feedback, and answer questions. In general, people tend to assume that talking to someone directly is more credible than receiving a written message. Face-to-face communication permits not only the exchange of words, but also the opportunity to see the nonverbal communication.

However, verbal communicating has its drawbacks. It can be inconsistent, unless all parties hear the same message. And although oral communication is useful for conveying the viewpoints of others and fostering an openness that encourages people to communicate, it is a weak tool for implementing a policy or issuing directives where many specifics are involved.

Here are two of the most important abilities for effective oral communication:

- **Active listening.** Listening is making sense of what is heard and requires paying attention, interpreting, and remembering sound stimuli. Effective listening is active, requiring the hearer to "get inside the head" of the speaker so that he or she can understand the communication from the speaker's point of view. Effective listeners do the following:

    Make eye contact.

    Schedule sufficient, uninterrupted time for meetings.

    Genuinely seek information.

    Avoid being emotional or attacking others.

Paraphrase the message you heard, especially to clarify the speaker's intentions.

Keep silent. Don't talk to fill pauses, or respond to statements in a point-counterpoint fashion.

Ask clarifying questions.

Avoid making distracting gestures.

■ **Constructive feedback.** Managers often do poor jobs of providing employees with performance feedback. When providing feedback, managers should do the following:

Focus on specific behaviors rather than making general statements

Keep feedback impersonal and goal-oriented

Offer feedback as soon after the action as possible

Ask questions to ensure understanding of the feedback

Direct negative feedback toward behavior that the recipient can control

Written communication skills

Written communication has several advantages. First, it provides a record for referral and follow-up. Second, written communication is an inexpensive means of providing identical messages to a large number of people.

The major limitation of written communication is that the sender does not know how or if the communication is received unless a reply is required.

Unfortunately, writing skills are often difficult to develop, and many individuals have problems writing simple, clear, and direct documents. And believe it or not, poorly written documents cost money.

How much does bad writing cost a company annually? According to a Canadian consulting and training firm, one employee who writes just one poorly worded memo per week over the course of a year can cost a company $4,258.60.

Managers must be able to write clearly. The ability to prepare letters, memos, sales reports, and other written documents may spell the difference between success and failure. The following are some guidelines for effective written communication:

- Use the P.O.W.E.R. Plan for preparing each message: plan, organize, write, edit, and revise

- Draft the message with the readers in mind

- Give the message a concise title and use subheadings where appropriate

- Use simple words and short, clear, sentences and paragraphs

- Back up opinions with facts

- Avoid "flowery" language, euphemisms, and trite expressions

- Summarize main points at the end and let the reader know what he must do next

Interpersonal Communication

Interpersonal communication is real-time, face-to-face or voice-to-voice conversation that allows immediate feedback. Interpersonal communication plays a large role in any manager's daily activities, but especially in organizations that use teams.

Managers must facilitate interpersonal communication within teams and reduce barriers to interpersonal communications. Common barriers to interpersonal communication include the following:

- **Expectations of familiarity** (or hearing what one is expected to hear). After hearing the beginning comments, employees may not listen to the remainder of the communication because they think they already know what a manager's going to say.

- **Preconceived notions.** Many employees ignore information that conflicts with what they "know." Often referred to as *selective perception,* it's the tendency to single out for attention those aspects of a situation or person that reinforce or appear consistent with one's existing beliefs, value, or needs. Selective perception can bias a manager's and employee's view of situations and people.

- **Source's lack of credibility.** Some employees may negatively size up or evaluate the sender based on stereotypes. *Stereotyping* is assigning attributes commonly associated with a category, such as age group, race, or gender to an individual. *Classifying* is making assumptions about an individual based on a group he or she fits into. Characteristics commonly associated with the group are then assigned to the individual. Someone who believes that young people dislike authority figures may assume that a younger colleague is rebellious.

■ **Differing perceptions caused by social and cultural backgrounds.** The process through which people receive and interpret information from the environment is called **perception.** Perception acts as a screen or filter through which information must pass before it has an impact on communication. The results of this screening process vary, because such things as values, cultural background, and other circumstances influence individual perceptions. Simply put, people can perceive the same things or situations very differently. And even more important, people behave according to their perceptions.

■ **Semantics and diction.** The choice and use of words differ significantly among individuals. A word such as "effectiveness" may mean "achieving high production" to a factory superintendent and "employee satisfaction" to a human resources specialist. Many common English words have an average of 28 definitions, so communicators must take care to select the words that accurately communicate their ideas.

■ **Emotions that interfere with reason.** Tempers often interfere with reason and cause the roles of sender and receiver to change to that of opponent and adversary.

■ **Noise or interference.** Noise does not allow for understanding between sender and receiver.

Organizational Communication

The formal flow of information in an organization may move via upward, downward, or horizontal channels. Most *downward communications* address plans, performance feedback, delegation, and training. Most *upward communications* concern performance, complaints, or requests for help. *Horizontal communications* focus on coordination of tasks or resources.

Organizational structure creates, perpetuates, and encourages formal means of communication. The chain of command typifies vertical communication. Teamwork and interactions exemplify lateral or horizontal efforts to communicate. Coordinating efforts between colleagues or employees of equal rank and authority represent this channel of communication. Feedback from subordinate to superior is indicative of upward communication.

For example, status reports to inform upper levels of management are originated in the lower or mid-range of most organizations.

The marriage of people to electronic communication equipment and databases that store information is a *formal network.* Formal communication networks provide the electronic links for transferring and storing information through formal organizational channels.

Informal channels, known as the grapevine, carry casual, social, and personal messages through the organization. The **grapevine** is an informal, person-to-person communication network of employees that is not officially sanctioned by the organization (see Chapter 3). The grapevine is spontaneous, quick, and hard to stop; it can both help and hinder the understanding of information. For these reasons, managers need to stay in touch with the grapevine and counteract rumors.

Like interpersonal communication, organizational communication can be blocked by barriers, such as the following:

- Information overload
- Embellished messages
- Delays in formal communications
- Lack of employee trust and openness
- Different styles of change
- Intimidation and unavailability of those of rank or status
- Manager's interpretations
- Electronic noises

Improving Communications

Communication touches everything that takes place in an organization and is so intermingled with all other functions and processes that separating it for study and analysis is difficult. Because communication is the most time-consuming activity that a manager engages in, improving management strongly depends on improving communication. One way researchers are trying to improve communication skills for organizations is through instruments that assess managers' writing and speaking effectiveness.

The responsibility to strengthen and improve communication is both individual and organizational. Senders should define the purpose behind their message, construct each message with the reader in mind, select the best medium, time each transmission thoughtfully, and seek feedback. Receivers must listen actively, be sensitive to the sender, recommend an appropriate medium for messages, and initiate feedback efforts.

Chapter Checkout

Q&A

1. Communication is complete when which of the following takes place?
   a. Verbal expression
   b. Face-to-face communication
   c. Written reply
   d. Mutual understanding

2. A return look of disdain without comment from an unhappy person may be interpreted as a
   a. verbal reply.
   b. stereotype.
   c. nonverbal communication.
   d. semantics.

3. "Guess what I just heard about the manager's new secretary?" typifies
   a. feedback.
   b. the grapevine.
   c. noise.
   d. downward communication.

Answers: 1. d **2.** c **3.** b

Chapter 14

CONTROL: THE LINKING FUNCTION

Chapter Check-In

❑ Relating control to the other four functions of management

❑ Understanding control as a process

❑ Knowing and using different controls

❑ Identifying an effective control system

Every manager in every organization today faces the dilemma of finding ways to administer and coordinate various processes—to control the activities under his or her jurisdiction. Managers continually look for ways to improve customer satisfaction, maintain relationships with suppliers, cut inventory costs, and develop the right products. As a result, every organization needs basic systems for allocating financial resources, developing human resources, analyzing financial performance, and evaluating overall profitability. Controlling is the management function in which managers establish and communicate performance standards for people, processes, and devices. In chapter 14, control system design, criteria for effective control, and basic control mechanisms are examined.

Control Objectives

Simply put, *organizational control* is the process of assigning, evaluating, and regulating resources on an ongoing basis to accomplish an organization's goals. To successfully control an organization, managers need to not only know what the performance standards are, but also figure out how to share that information with employees.

Control can be defined narrowly as the process a manager takes to assure that actual performance conforms to the organization's plan, or more broadly as anything that regulates the process or activity of an organization. The content in this chapter follows the general interpretation by defining managerial control as monitoring performance against a plan and then making adjustments either in the plan or in operations as necessary.

The six major purposes of controls are as follows:

- **Controls make plans effective.** Managers need to measure progress, offer feedback, and direct their teams if they want to succeed.

- **Controls make sure that organizational activities are consistent.** Policies and procedures help ensure that efforts are integrated.

- **Controls make organizations effective.** Organizations need controls in place if they want to achieve and accomplish their objectives.

- **Controls make organizations efficient.** Efficiency probably depends more on controls than any other management function.

- **Controls provide feedback on project status.** Not only do they measure progress, but controls also provide feedback to participants as well. Feedback influences behavior and is an essential ingredient in the control process.

- **Controls aid in decision making.** The ultimate purpose of controls is to help managers make better decisions. Controls make managers aware of problems and give them information that is necessary for decision making.

Many people assert that as the nature of organizations has changed, so must the nature of management controls. New forms of organizations, such as self-organizing organizations, self-managed teams, and network organizations, allow organizations to be more responsive and adaptable in today's rapidly changing world. These forms also cultivate empowerment among employees, much more so than the hierarchical organizations of the past.

Some people even claim that management shouldn't exercise any form of control whatsoever, and should only support employee efforts to be fully productive members of organizations and communities. Along those same lines, some experts even use the word "coordinating" in place of "controlling" to avoid sounding coercive. However, some forms of controls must exist for an organization to exist. For an organization to exist, it needs some goal or purpose, or it isn't an organization at all. Individual behaviors, group behaviors, and all organizational performance must be in line with the strategic focus of the organization.

The Control Process

The control process involves carefully collecting information about a system, process, person, or group of people in order to make necessary decisions about each. Managers set up control systems that consist of four key steps:

1. **Establish standards to measure performance.** Within an organization's overall strategic plan, managers define goals for organizational departments in specific, operational terms that include standards of performance to compare with organizational activities.

2. **Measure actual performance.** Most organizations prepare formal reports of performance measurements that managers review regularly. These measurements should be related to the standards set in the first step of the control process. For example, if sales growth is a target, the organization should have a means of gathering and reporting sales data.

3. **Compare performance with the standards.** This step compares actual activities to performance standards. When managers read computer reports or walk through their plants, they identify whether actual performance meets, exceeds, or falls short of standards. Typically, performance reports simplify such comparison by placing the performance standards for the reporting period alongside the actual performance for the same period and by computing the variance—that is, the difference between each actual amount and the associated standard.

4. **Take corrective actions.** When performance deviates from standards, managers must determine what changes, if any, are necessary and how to apply them. In the productivity and quality-centered environment (see Chapter 15 for more information), workers and managers are often empowered to evaluate their own work. After the evaluator determines the cause or causes of deviation, he or she can take the fourth step—corrective action. The most effective course may be prescribed by policies or may be best left up to employees' judgment and initiative.

These steps must be repeated periodically until the organizational goal is achieved.

Types of Controls

Control can focus on events before, during, or after a process. For example, a local automobile dealer can focus on activities before, during, or after sales of new cars. Careful inspection of new cars and cautious selection of sales employees are ways to ensure high quality or profitable sales even before those sales take place. Monitoring how salespeople act with customers is a control during the sales task. Counting the number of new cars sold during the month and telephoning buyers about their satisfaction with sales transactions are controls after sales have occurred. These types of controls are formally called feedforward, concurrent, and feedback, respectively.

- **Feedforward controls,** sometimes called preliminary or preventive controls, attempt to identify and prevent deviations in the standards before they occur. Feedforward controls focus on human, material, and financial resources within the organization. These controls are evident in the selection and hiring of new employees. For example, organizations attempt to improve the likelihood that employees will perform up to standards by identifying the necessary job skills and by using tests and other screening devices to hire people with those skills.

- **Concurrent controls** monitor ongoing employee activity to ensure consistency with quality standards. These controls rely on performance standards, rules, and regulations for guiding employee tasks and behaviors. Their purpose is to ensure that work activities produce the desired results. As an example, many manufacturing operations include devices that measure whether the items being produced meet quality standards. Employees monitor the measurements; if they see that standards are not being met in some area, they make a correction themselves or let a manager know that a problem is occurring.

- **Feedback controls** involve reviewing information to determine whether performance meets established standards. For example, suppose that an organization establishes a goal of increasing its profit by 12 percent next year. To ensure that this goal is reached, the organization must monitor its profit on a monthly basis. After three months, if profit has increased by 3 percent, management might assume that plans are going according to schedule.

Characteristics of Effective Control Systems

The management of any organization must develop a control system tailored to its organization's goals and resources. Effective control systems share several common characteristics. These characteristics are as follows:

- **A focus on critical points.** For example, controls are applied where failure cannot be tolerated or where costs cannot exceed a certain amount. The critical points include all the areas of an organization's operations that directly affect the success of its key operations.

- **Integration into established processes.** Controls must function harmoniously within these processes and should not bottleneck operations.

- **Acceptance by employees.** Employee involvement in the design of controls can increase acceptance.

- **Availability of information when needed.** Deadlines, time needed to complete the project, costs associated with the project, and priority needs are apparent in these criteria. Costs are frequently attributed to time shortcomings or failures.

- **Economic feasibility.** Effective control systems answer questions such as, "How much does it cost?" "What will it save?" or "What are the returns on the investment?" In short, comparison of the costs to the benefits ensures that the benefits of controls outweigh the costs.

- **Accuracy.** Effective control systems provide factual information that's useful, reliable, valid, and consistent.

- **Comprehensibility.** Controls must be simple and easy to understand.

Control Techniques

Control techniques provide managers with the type and amount of information they need to measure and monitor performance. The information from various controls must be tailored to a specific management level, department, unit, or operation.

To ensure complete and consistent information, organizations often use standardized documents such as financial, status, and project reports. Each area within an organization, however, uses its own specific control techniques, described in the following sections.

Financial controls

After the organization has strategies in place to reach its goals, funds are set aside for the necessary resources and labor. As money is spent, statements are updated to reflect how much was spent, how it was spent, and what it obtained. Managers use these financial statements, such as an income statement or balance sheet, to monitor the progress of programs and plans. **Financial statements** provide management with information to monitor financial resources and activities. The **income statement** shows the results of the organization's operations over a period of time, such as revenues, expenses, and profit or loss. The *balance sheet* shows what the organization is worth (assets) at a single point in time, and the extent to which those assets were financed through debt (liabilities) or owner's investment (equity).

Financial audits, or formal investigations, are regularly conducted to ensure that financial management practices follow generally accepted procedures, policies, laws, and ethical guidelines. Audits may be conducted internally or externally. **Financial ratio analysis** examines the relationship between specific figures on the financial statements and helps explain the significance of those figures:

- **Liquidity ratios** measure an organization's ability to generate cash.

- **Profitability ratios** measure an organization's ability to generate profits.

- **Debt ratios** measure an organization's ability to pay its debts.

- **Activity ratios** measure an organization's efficiency in operations and use of assets.

In addition, *financial responsibility centers* require managers to account for a unit's progress toward financial goals within the scope of their influences. A manager's goals and responsibilities may focus on unit profits, costs, revenues, or investments.

Budget controls

A budget depicts how much an organization expects to spend (expenses) and earn (revenues) over a time period. Amounts are categorized according to the type of business activity or account, such as telephone costs or sales of catalogs. Budgets not only help managers plan their finances, but also help them keep track of their overall spending.

A budget, in reality, is both a planning tool and a control mechanism. Budget development processes vary among organizations according to who does the budgeting and how the financial resources are allocated. Some budget development methods are as follows:

- **Top-down budgeting.** Managers prepare the budget and send it to subordinates.

- **Bottom-up budgeting.** Figures come from the lower levels and are adjusted and coordinated as they move up the hierarchy.

- **Zero-based budgeting.** Managers develop each new budget by justifying the projected allocation against its contribution to departmental or organizational goals.

- **Flexible budgeting.** Any budget exercise can incorporate flexible budgets, which set "meet or beat" standards that can be compared to expenditures.

Marketing controls

Marketing controls help monitor progress toward goals for customer satisfaction with products and services, prices, and delivery. The following are examples of controls used to evaluate an organization's marketing functions:

- **Market research** gathers data to assess customer needs—information critical to an organization's success. Ongoing market research reflects how well an organization is meeting customers' expectations and helps anticipate customer needs. It also helps identify competitors.

- **Test marketing** is small-scale product marketing to assess customer acceptance. Using surveys and focus groups, test marketing goes beyond identifying general requirements and looks at what (or who) actually influences buying decisions.

- **Marketing statistics** measure performance by compiling data and analyzing results. In most cases, competency with a computer spreadsheet program is all a manager needs. Managers look at *marketing ratios,* which measure profitability, activity, and market shares, as well as *sales quotas,* which measure progress toward sales goals and assist with inventory controls.

Unfortunately, scheduling a regular evaluation of an organization's marketing program is easier to recommend than to execute. Usually, only a crisis, such as increased competition or a sales drop, forces a company to take a closer look at its marketing program. However, more regular evaluations help minimize the number of marketing problems.

Human resource controls

Human resource controls help managers regulate the quality of newly hired personnel, as well as monitor current employees' developments and daily performances.

On a daily basis, managers can go a long way in helping to control workers' behaviors in organizations. They can help direct workers' performances toward goals by making sure that goals are clearly set and understood. Managers can also institute policies and procedures to help guide workers' actions. Finally, they can consider past experiences when developing future strategies, objectives, policies, and procedures.

Common control types include performance appraisals, disciplinary programs, observations, and training and development assessments. Because the quality of a firm's personnel, to a large degree, determines the firm's overall effectiveness, controlling this area is very crucial. Human resource management is discussed in Chapter 9.

Computers and information controls

Almost all organizations have confidential and sensitive information that they don't want to become general knowledge. Controlling access to computer databases is the key to this area.

Increasingly, computers are being used to collect and store information for control purposes. Many organizations privately monitor each employee's computer usage to measure employee performance, among other things. Some people question the appropriateness of computer monitoring. Managers must carefully weigh the benefits against the costs—both human and financial—before investing in and implementing computerized control techniques.

Although computers and information systems provide enormous benefits, such as improved productivity and information management, organizations should remember the following limitations of the use of information technology:

- **Performance limitations.** Although management information systems have the potential to increase overall performance, replacing long-time organizational employees with information systems technology may result in the loss of expert knowledge that these individuals hold. Additionally, computerized information systems are expensive and difficult to develop. After the system has been purchased, coordinating it—possibly with existing equipment—may be more difficult than expected. Consequently, a company may cut corners or install the system carelessly to the detriment of the system's performance and utility. And like other sophisticated electronic equipment, information systems do not work all the time, resulting in costly downtime.

■ **Behavioral limitations.** Information technology allows managers to access more information than ever before. But too much information can overwhelm employees, cause stress, and even slow decision making. Thus, managing the quality and amount of information available to avoid information overload is important.

■ **Health risks.** Potentially serious health-related issues associated with the use of computers and other information technology have been raised in recent years. An example is carpal tunnel syndrome, a painful disorder in the hands and wrists caused by repetitive movements (such as those made on a keyboard).

Regardless of the control processes used, an effective system determines whether employees and various parts of an organization are on target in achieving organizational objectives.

Chapter Checkout

Q&A

1. The objectives that eventually determine the selection of control methods are developed during what function?
   a. Planning
   b. Organizing
   c. Staffing
   d. Leading

2. The control process requires managers to establish standards for performance, measure performance against those standards, and
   a. know their organization's mission.
   b. establish technical standards.
   c. take necessary actions to correct deviations.
   d. control unexpected situations.

3. Which of the following are the three basic types of controls?

   a. Prevention, diagnostic, and therapeutic

   b. Feedforward, in-process, and diagnostic

   c. Prevention, feedback, and feedforward

   d. Feedforward, concurrent, and feedback

4. A budget is purposefully designed as what type of control to provide summary information to management?

   a. Prevention

   b. Feedback

   c. Feedforward

   d. Concurrent

5. Performance appraisals are a part of what type of controls?

   a. Accounting

   b. Human resource

   c. Inventory

   d. Financial

Answers: 1. a **2.** c **3.** d **4.** d **5.** b.

Chapter 15

IMPROVING PRODUCTIVITY THROUGH TOTAL QUALITY MANAGEMENT

Chapter Check-In

❑ Understanding the significance of productivity and quality

❑ Defining total quality management

❑ Learning from the authorities about total quality management

❑ Relating total quality management concepts to consumers

❑ Implementing total quality management

Business leaders have long been seeking a magic formula for success in the global marketplace. During the past two decades, the quality of goods and services in the United States and the apparent decline in international competitiveness of many U.S. firms has become a hot topic. The business community is inundated with calls for the improved quality of American goods and services.

Quality reflects the degree to which a good or service meets the demands and requirements of the marketplace. It is an elusive concept whose definition differs according to the type of organization involved. To an appliance manufacturer, for example, quality might mean that a very high percentage of the appliances produced meet predetermined specifications. To an appliance repair business, quality might mean that products are repaired correctly within stated cost and deadline parameters. To a fast-food service firm such as McDonald's, quality applies to both the food itself (taste, freshness, and so on) and the service (length of time to be served, friendliness of the cashier, cleanliness of dining room, and so on).

In this chapter, one approach to improving the quality of goods and services in an organization is discussed: Total Quality Management.

Productivity and Quality

After companies determine customer needs, they must concentrate on meeting those needs by yielding high quality products at an efficient rate. Companies can improve quality and productivity by securing the commitments of all three levels of management and employees as follows:

- **Top-level management:** Implement sound management practices, use research and development effectively, adopt modern manufacturing techniques, and improve time management.

- **Middle management:** Plan and coordinate quality and productivity efforts.

- **Low-level management:** Work with employees to improve productivity through acceptance of change, commitment to quality, and continually improving all facets of their work.

Productivity is the relationship between a given amount of output and the amount of input needed to produce it. Profitability results when money is left over from sales after costs are paid. The expenditures made to ensure that the product or service meets quality specifications affect the final or overall cost of the products and/or services involved. Efficiency of costs will be an important consideration in all stages of the market system from manufacturing to consumption. Quality affects productivity. Both affect profitability. The drive for any one of the three must not interfere with the drive for the others. Efforts at improvement need to be coordinated and integrated. The real cost of quality is the cost of avoiding nonconformance and failure. Another cost is the cost of not having quality—of losing customers and wasting resources.

As long as companies continually interact with their customers and various partners, and develop learning relationships between all levels of management and employees, the levels of productivity and quality should remain high.

Total Quality Management

Total Quality Management (TQM) is a philosophy that says that uniform commitment to quality in all areas of an organization promotes an organizational culture that meets consumers' perceptions of quality.

The concept of TQM rests largely on five principles:

1. Produce quality work the first time.
2. Focus on the customer.
3. Have a strategic approach to improvement.
4. Improve continuously.
5. Encourage mutual respect and teamwork.

To be effective in improving quality, TQM must be supported at all levels of a firm, from the highest executive to the lowest-level hourly employee. TQM extends the definition of quality to all functional areas of the organization, including production, marketing, finance, and information systems. The process begins by listening to customers' wants and needs and then delivering goods and services that fulfill these desires. TQM even expands the definition of customer to include any person inside or outside the company to whom an employee passes his or her work. In a restaurant, for example, the cooks' customers are the waiters and waitresses. This notion encourages each member of the organization to stay focused on quality and remain fully aware of his or her contribution to it and responsibility for it.

The TQM philosophy focuses on teamwork, increasing customer satisfaction, and lowering costs. Organizations implement TQM by encouraging managers and employees to collaborate across functions and departments, as well as with customers and suppliers, to identify areas for improvement, no matter how small. Teams of workers are trained and empowered to make decisions that help their organization achieve high standards of quality. Organizations shift responsibility for quality control from specialized departments to all employees. Thus, total quality management means a shift from a bureaucratic to a decentralized approach to control.

An effective TQM program has numerous benefits. Financial benefits include lower costs, higher returns on sales and investment, and the ability to charge higher rather than competitive prices. Other benefits include improved access to global markets, higher customer retention levels, less time required to develop new innovations, and a reputation as a quality firm. Only a small number of companies use TQM because implementing an effective program involves much time, effort, money, and patience. However, firms with the necessary resources may gain major competitive advantages in their industries by implementing TQM.

Major Contributors

Total quality management is a much broader concept than just controlling the quality of the product itself. Total quality management is the coordination of efforts directed at improving customer satisfaction, increasing employee participation, strengthening supplier partnerships, and facilitating an organizational atmosphere of continuous quality improvement. TQM is a way of thinking about organizations and how people should relate and work in them. TQM is not merely a technique, but a philosophy anchored in the belief that long-term success depends on a uniform commitment to quality in all sectors of an organization. In the following sections, the significant contributors to TQM are discussed.

W. Edwards Deming

The concept of quality started in Japan when the country began to rebuild after World War II. Amidst the bomb rubble, Japan embraced the ideas of W. Edwards Deming, an American whose methods and theories are credited for Japan's postwar recovery. Ironically enough, Deming's ideas were initially scoffed at in the U.S. As a result, TQM took root in Japan 30 years earlier than in the United States. American companies took interest in Deming's ideas only when they began having trouble competing with the Japanese in the 1980s.

Deming's management system was philosophical, based on continuous improvement toward the perfect ideal. He believed that a commitment to quality requires transforming the entire organization. His philosophy is based on a system known as the Fourteen Points. These points express the actions an organization must take in order to achieve TQM:

1. **Create constancy of purpose for improvement of product and service.** Dr. Deming suggests a radical new definition of a company's role: A better way to make money is to stay in business and provide jobs through innovation, research, constant improvement, and maintenance.

2. **Adopt a new philosophy.** For the new economic age, companies need to change into "learning organizations." Furthermore, we need a new belief in which mistakes and negativism are unacceptable.

3. **Cease dependence on mass inspection.** Eliminate the need for mass inspection by building quality into the product.

4. **End awarding business on price.** Instead, aim at minimum total cost, and move towards single suppliers.

5. **Improve the system of production and service constantly.** Improvement is not a one-time effort. Management is obligated to continually look for ways to reduce waste and improve quality.

6. **Institute training.** Too often, workers learn their jobs from other workers who have never been trained properly.

7. **Institute leadership.** Leading consists of helping people to do a better job and to learn by objective methods.

8. **Drive out fear.** Many employees are afraid to ask questions or to take a position—even when they do not understand what their job is or what is right or wrong. The economic losses from fear are appalling. To assure better quality and productivity, it is necessary that people feel secure.

9. **Break down barriers between departments.** Often, company departments or units compete with each other or have goals that conflict. They do not work as a team; therefore they cannot solve or foresee problems. Even worse, one department's goal may cause trouble for another.

10. **Eliminate slogans, exhortations, and numerical targets for the workforce.** These never help anybody do a good job. Let workers formulate their own slogans; then they will be committed to the contents.

11. **Eliminate numerical quotas or work standards.** Quotas take into account only numbers, not quality or methods. They are usually a guarantee of inefficiency and high cost.

12. **Remove barriers that prevent workers from taking pride in their workmanship.** Too often, misguided supervisors, faulty equipment, and defective materials stand in the way of good performance. These barriers must be removed.

13. **Institute a vigorous program of education.** Both management and the work force will have to be informed of new knowledge and techniques.

14. **Take action to accomplish the transformation.** It will require a special top management team with a plan of action to carry out the quality mission. Workers cannot do it on their own, nor can managers. A critical mass of people in the company must understand the Fourteen Points.

Deming emphasized surveying customers, consulting production-line workers to help solve quality problems, and teamwork. His system was readily accepted in Japan, where workers and management were used to uniformity and allegiance to institutions. Japanese companies learned to collect data for the statistical monitoring and measuring of customer satisfaction. The goals of these companies were to produce many of the same consumer goods— better and cheaper—that were produced in the U.S. These Japanese companies succeeded, much to the chagrin of companies in the U.S.

Deming saw businesses as bedrock institutions in a society—much like churches and schools. Companies attain long-term success only if business leaders make their employees' contributions matter. If organizations use their employees' ideas, they will improve efficiency and productivity.

Most of the applications of Deming's ideas occurred in the 1950s and 1960s in Japan. In the United States, the desperation needed for executives to finally try a "radical" plan such as Deming's came from economic rather than wartime defeats. Most notably, in the 1980s, Japanese car manufacturers pushed their market share toward 25 percent, sending fear throughout Detroit. The Ford Motor Co. called on Deming after NBC featured his successes in a documentary, "If Japan Can, Why Can't We?" Deming took Ford's invitation as notice that his home country was finally ready for his program. He continued teaching seminars until his death, at age 93, in 1993.

Deming's system made such an impression that he is known at the Father of TQM.

Following are some other significant quality experts and their works:

- **Joseph M. Juran** wrote *The Quality Control Handbook*. Recognized in Japan with the Order of Sacred Treasure. Followers: DuPont, Monsanto, Mobil.

- **Armand V. Feigenbaum** wrote *Total Quality Control*. Argued that quality should be company-wide, not confined to the quality control departments.

- **Philip B. Crosby** wrote *Quality Is Free*.

- **Michael Hammer and James Champy** wrote *Reengineering the Corporation*.

- **James Champy** wrote *Reengineering Management*.

- **Peter Drucker** wrote *Post-Capitalist Society*.

Although several individuals (mentioned above) contributed to the concept of TQM, the three mostly widely cited "masters" of quality are W. Edwards Deming (1900–1993), Joseph M. Juran, and Philip Crosby.

Even though each has promoted the importance of quality emphasis, their ideas and backgrounds are not always consistent.

Joseph Juran

Joseph Juran started out professionally as an engineer in 1924. In 1951, his first Quality Control Handbook was published and led him to international prominence.

The Union of Japanese Scientists and Engineers (JUSE) invited Juran to Japan in the early 1950s. He arrived in 1954 and conducted seminars for top- and middle-level executives. His lectures had a strong managerial flavor and focused on planning, organizational issues, management's responsibility for quality, and the need to set goals and targets for improvement. He emphasized that quality control should be conducted as an integral part of management control.

Intrinsic to Juran's message is the belief that quality does not happen by accident; it must be planned. Juran sees quality planning as part of the quality trilogy of quality planning, quality control, and quality improvement. The key elements in implementing company-wide strategic quality planning are in turn seen as: identifying customers and their needs; establishing optimal quality goals; creating measurements of quality; planning processes capable of meeting quality goals under operating conditions; and producing continuing results in improved market share, premium prices, and a reduction of error rates in the office and factory.

Juran's formula for results is to establish specific goals to be reached, and then to establish plans for reaching those goals; assign clear responsibility for meeting the goals; and base the rewards on results achieved.

Juran believes that the majority of quality problems are the fault of poor management, not poor workmanship, and that long-term training to improve quality should start at the top with senior management.

Philip Crosby

Philip Crosby is another major contributor to the quality movement. In 1979, he left ITT (International Telephone and Telegraph) and wrote his book, *Quality is Free,* in which he argues that dollars spent on quality and the attention paid to it always return greater benefits than the costs expended on them. Whereas Deming and Juran emphasized the sacrifice required for a quality commitment, Crosby takes a less philosophical and more practical approach, asserting instead that high quality is relatively easy and inexpensive in the long run.

Crosby is the only American quality expert without a doctorate. He is responsible for the **zero defects** program, which emphasizes "doing it right the first time," (DIRFT) with 100 percent acceptable output. Unlike Deming and Juran, Crosby argues that quality is always cost effective. Like Deming and Juran, Crosby does not place the blame on workers, but on management.

Crosby also developed a 14-point program, which is again more practical than philosophical. It provides managers with actual concepts that can help them manage productivity and quality. His program is built around four Absolutes of Quality Management:

1. Quality must be viewed as conformance to specifications. If a product meets design specifications, then it is a high-quality product.

2. Quality should be achieved through the prevention of defects rather than inspection after the production process is complete.

   According to Crosby, the traditional quality control approach taken by American firms is not cost effective. Instead, production workers should be granted the authority and responsibility to ensure that quality goods or services are produced at every step of the process.

3. Managers need to demonstrate that a higher standard of performance can lead to perfection—to zero defects. Crosby believed that the company goal should be zero defects.

4. Quality should be measured by the price of nonconformity. Crosby contends that the costs associated with achieving quality should be part of a company's financial system.

The Implementation of TQM

The implementation of total quality management is similar to that of other decentralized control methods (see Chapter 14). In developing TQM, companies need to understand how consumers define quality in both the goods and services offered. If a company pays more attention to quality in its production process, fewer problems will occur later when the product is in the consumer's hands. One way to measure product performance and quality is through customer surveys, which can help managers identify design or manufacturing problems.

According to quality consultant Armand V. Feigenbaum, the end user best defines quality, which means that quality is open to subjective interpretations. Consumer perceptions have to be changed if a company wants to change a product's quality image. Extended service programs and improved warranties can help accomplish this feat. As examples, Whirlpool Corporation promises that parts for all models will be available for 15 years, and Mercedes-Benz provides technical roadside assistance after dealer service hours.

Another means of ensuring a commitment to quality "after the sale" is via a product or service guarantee. Wal-Mart is known for its no-hassles return policy for any product—with or without a receipt. Mail-order house L. L. Bean will replace a pair of hunting boots purchased ten years earlier with new boots. Saturn automobile retailers provide total refunds for vehicles within 30 days if the customer is not fully satisfied. However, many companies are not willing to incur the short-run costs associated with such guarantees.

Commitment throughout the organization

To be effective, the TQM philosophy must begin at the top. From the board of directors to the hourly line employees, TQM must be supported at all levels if the firm is to realize any real improvements in quality. In addition to commitment from the top, the organization must meet these requirements if TQM is to succeed:

- A change in corporate culture about the importance of quality

- Forging of internal team partnerships to achieve quality, process, and project improvements, and the creation of external partnerships with customers and suppliers

- Audits to assure quality techniques

- Removal of obstacles to successful implementation, such as lack of time or money in the short run

Typically, two to ten years are needed to reap the benefits of a successful TQM program.

World-Class Quality: ISO 9000 Certification

With the highly competitive nature of the current business world, customers can dictate who, what, when, where, why, and how much regarding market commodities and services. In other words, quality has never counted more. As a result, management and organizations must heed these calls and specifically cater to the ever-changing expectations of their international clientele.

Globally, customers expect quality whether they are buying a consumer product or receiving a service. As a result, many countries have adopted the quality standards set by the International Standards Organization (ISO) in Geneva, Switzerland.

Businesses that want to compete as world-class companies are increasingly expected to have *ISO 9000 Certification* at various levels. To gain certification in this family of quality standards, businesses must undergo a rigorous assessment by outside auditors to determine whether they meet ISO requirements. Increasingly, the ISO stamp of approval is viewed as a necessity in international business; the ISO certification provides customers with an assurance that a set of solid quality standards and processes are in place.

The commitment to total quality operations is now a way of life in world-class firms. In the United States, the Malcolm Baldridge National Quality Awards were established to benchmark excellence in quality achievements. The following list of award criteria indicates the full extent of the day-to-day commitment that is essential to gaining competitive advantage through a commitment to total quality:

- Top executives incorporate quality values into day-to-day management.

- The organization works with suppliers to improve the quality of their goods and/or services.

- The organization trains workers in quality techniques and implements systems that ensure high-quality products.

- The organization's products are as good as or better than those of its competitors.

- The organization meets customers' needs and wants and gets customer satisfaction ratings equal to or better than those of competitors.

- The organization's quality system yields concrete results such as increased market share and lower product cycle times.

Chapter Checkout

Q&A

1. The leading and recognized intellectual gurus of TQM include all of the following except

- **a.** Philip B. Crosby
- **b.** Joseph M. Juran
- **c.** W. Edwards Deming
- **d.** William Dirft

2. In an effort to be successful, organizations must champion total quality management

- **a.** at lower management exclusively.
- **b.** mostly toward top management.
- **c.** toward all levels of management and employees.
- **d.** to suppliers only.

3. Which TQM advocate authored the Fourteen Points of improvement regarding quality control?

- **a.** Walter R. Shewhart
- **b.** Philip B. Crosby
- **c.** W. Edwards Deming
- **d.** Joseph M. Juran

4. An undaunted acceptance and commitment for total quality management means that people must do which of the following?

- **a.** Change
- **b.** Energize
- **c.** Behave
- **d.** Dominate

5. Within the TQM environment, suppliers and customers are thought of as what kind of partners?

- **a.** Controllable
- **b.** External
- **c.** Demanding
- **d.** Buying

Answers: 1. d 2. c 3. c 4. a 5. b.

Chapter 16

MANAGEMENT IN A GLOBAL ENVIRONMENT

Chapter Check-In

❑ Understanding how companies evolve internationally

❑ Examining multinational firms

❑ Assessing environmental differences

❑ Managing in the international business world

Since the early 1970s, the U.S. has seen a tremendous amount of foreign competition in virtually every product and service industry. Russia and Eastern European countries are entering the international marketplace as they convert their socialist economies to capitalism and trade barriers continue to fall. All over the world, the global marketplace has opened up new competition for any organization in any country to join.

To remain viable and competitive, organizations must be prepared to compete in world markets. Global expansion offers the greatest opportunities for growth. In this chapter, the various environments that affect an organization's success in a foreign country are discussed. In addition, the changes in management functions and personal challenges that come about when working in an international company are addressed.

The Multinational Corporation

In the period after World War One, America fell under the sway of "America First" thinking. In 1929, a great financial disaster occurred, and America suffered its worst depression. At first, laissez faire economic methods were adopted, but with the election of Franklin Roosevelt, a British economist's theories were tried. John Maynard Keynes came up with the idea that government should "prime the pump" of the national economy with spending programs. It seemed to work. After World War II, America took the opposite approach and helped its world neighbors rebuild their economies.

The die was cast for more international involvement. Before many years had passed, American companies had invested money in many foreign lands. Revlon, Coca-Cola, GM, most of the oil companies, and even major banks all had large international operations.

If a company wants to venture into the international marketplace, it can use several different methods. In each case, the levels of risk and control move together. The four most common approaches include the following:

- **Exporting.** The selling of an organization's products to a foreign broker or agent is known as **exporting.** The organization has virtually no control over how products are marketed after the foreign broker or agent purchases them. Because the investment is relatively small, exporting is a low-risk method of entering foreign markets. The only real danger here is what the foreign agent might do with the products to hurt the organization's or product's image.

- **Licensure agreement.** This approach allows a foreign firm to either manufacture or sell products, or the right to place a brand name or symbols on products. Disney World, for example, has licensure agreements with many foreign firms. This approach provides more control than an export sale, as a firm can require that certain specifications be met, yet it is still not the manufacturer in the foreign market.

- **Multinational approach.** With this approach, a firm is willing to make substantial commitment to a foreign market. Normally, products or services are modified to meet the foreign market demands, and in many cases, substantial fixed investments are made in plants and equipment. The most common ways to become a multinational firm are to form joint ventures or global strategic partnerships, or to establish wholly-owned subsidiaries.

    Joint ventures occur when a company forms a partnership with a foreign firm to develop new products or to give each other access to local markets. Normally, the roles and responsibilities of each organization are clearly spelled out in the joint-venture agreement. This approach increases both control and risk.

Global strategic partnerships are much larger than a simple joint venture. Two firms join together and make a long-term commitment, in the form of time and investments, to develop products or services that will dominate world markets. This approach does not modify products for a particular market but develops a single product market strategy that can be utilized in all markets in hopes of dominating the worldwide market for that product.

Wholly-owned subsidiaries occur when a firm purchases either controlling interest or all of a foreign firm. Often, the subsidiary firm is given considerable freedom in terms of how to operate in the foreign market, and heavy use of foreign managers and employees is very common. The owning firm does have the most control, but it also has substantial investment risk.

Vertically integrated wholly-owned subsidiaries exist where a firm owns not only the foreign manufacturer but the foreign distributors and retailers as well. Again, the main emphasis is on dominating a worldwide product or service area with a single product market strategy. True global products are very difficult to develop, and it is even more difficult to dominate all global markets.

Of these approaches, **multinational corporations,** defined as organizations operating facilities in one or more countries, are major forces in the movement toward the globalization of businesses. Common characteristics of successful multinational corporations include the following:

- Creation of foreign affiliates

- Global visions and strategies

- Engagement in manufacturing or in a restricted number of industries

- Location in developed countries

- Adoption of high-skills staffing strategies, cheap labor strategies, or a mixture of both.

The next section discusses in detail the various issues that an international manager faces.

The International Environment

International managers face intense and constant challenges that require training and understanding of the foreign environment. Managing a business in a foreign country requires managers to deal with a large variety of cultural and environmental differences. As a result, international managers must continually monitor the political, legal, sociocultural, economic, and technological environments.

The political environment

The political environment can foster or hinder economic developments and direct investments. This environment is ever-changing. As examples, the political and economic philosophies of a nation's leader may change overnight. The stability of a nation's government, which frequently rests on the support of the people, can be very volatile. Various citizen groups with vested interests can undermine investment operations and opportunities. And local governments may view foreign firms suspiciously.

Political considerations are seldom written down and often change rapidly. For example, to protest Iraq's invasion of Kuwait in 1990, many world governments levied economic sanctions against the import of Iraqi oil. Political considerations affect international business daily as governments enact **tariffs** (taxes), **quotas** (annual limits), **embargoes** (blockages), and other types of restriction in response to political events.

Businesses engaged in international trade must consider the relative instability of countries such as Iraq, South Africa, and Honduras. Political unrest in countries such as Peru, Haiti, Somalia, and the countries of the former Soviet Union may create hostile or even dangerous environments for foreign businesses. In Russia, for example, foreign managers often need to hire bodyguards; sixteen foreign businesspeople were murdered there in 1993. Civil war, as in Chechnya and Bosnia, may disrupt business activities and place lives in danger. And a sudden change in power can result in a regime that is hostile to foreign investment; some businesses may be forced out of a country altogether. Whether they like it or not, companies are often involved directly or indirectly in international politics.

The legal enviroment

The American federal government has put forth a number of laws that regulate the activities of U.S. firms engaged in international trade. However, once outside U.S. borders, American organizations are likely to find that the laws of the other nations differ from those of the U.S. Many legal rights that Americans take for granted do not exist in other countries; a U.S. firm doing business abroad must understand and obey the laws of the host country.

In the U.S., the acceptance of bribes or payoffs is illegal; in other countries, the acceptance of bribes or payoffs may not be illegal—they may be considered a common business practice. In addition, some countries have copyright and patent laws that are less strict than those in the U.S., and some countries fail to honor these laws. China, for example, has recently been threatened with severe trade sanctions because of a history of allowing American goods to be copied or counterfeited there. As a result, businesses engaging in international trade may need to take extra steps to protect their products because local laws may be insufficient to protect them.

The economic environment

Managers must monitor currency, infrastructure, inflation, interest rates, wages, and taxation. In assessing the economic environment in foreign countries, a business must pay particular attention to the following four areas:

■ **Average income levels of the population.** If the average income for the population is very low, no matter how desperately this population needs a product or service, there simply is not a market for it.

■ **Tax structures.** In some countries, foreign firms pay much higher tax rates than domestic competitors. These tax differences may be very obvious or subtle, as in hidden registration fees.

■ **Inflation rates.** In the U.S., for example, inflation rates have been quite low and relatively stable for several years. In some countries, however, inflation rates of 30, 40, or even 100 percent per year are not uncommon. Inflation results in a general rise in the level of prices and impacts business in many ways. For example, in the mid-1970s, a shortage of crude oil led to numerous problems because petroleum products supply most of the energy required to produce goods and services and to transport goods around the world. As the cost of petroleum products increased, a corresponding increase took place in the cost of goods and services. As a result, interest rates increased dramatically, causing both businesses and consumers to reduce their borrowing. Business profits fell as consumers' purchasing power was eroded by inflation. High interest rates and unemployment reached alarmingly high levels.

■ **Fluctuating exchange rates.** The *exchange rate,* or the value of one country's currency in terms of another country's currency, is determined primarily by supply and demand for each country's goods and services. The government of a country can, however, cause this exchange rate to change dramatically by causing high inflation—by printing too much currency or by changing the value of the currency through devaluation. A foreign investor may sustain large losses if the value of the currency drops substantially.

When doing business abroad, businesspeople need to recognize that they cannot take for granted that other countries offer the same things as are found in industrialized nations. A country's level of development is often determined in part by its infrastructure. The **infrastructure** is the physical facilities that support a country's economic activities, such as railroads, highways, ports, utilities and power plants, schools, hospitals, communication systems, and commercial distribution systems. When doing business in less developed countries, a business may need to compensate for rudimentary distribution and communication systems.

The sociocultural environment

Cultural differences, which can be very subtle, are extremely important. An organization that enters the international marketplace on virtually any level must make learning the foreign country's cultural taboos and proper cultural practices a high priority. If a business fails to understand the cultural methods of doing business, grave misunderstandings and a complete lack of trust may occur.

Management differences also exist. In China, a harmonious environment is more important than day-to-day productivity. In Morocco, women can assume leadership roles, but they are usually more self-conscious than American women. In Pakistan, women are not often found in management positions, if they're in the workplace at all.

In addition, the importance of work in employees' lives varies from country to country. For example, the Japanese feel that work is an important part of their lives. This belief in work, coupled with a strong group orientation, may explain the Japanese willingness to put up with things that workers in other countries would find intolerable.

Likewise, culture may impact what employees find motivating, as well as how they respond to rewards and punishments. For example, Americans tend to emphasize personal growth, accomplishment, and "getting what you deserve" for performance as the most important motivators. However, in Asian cultures, maintaining group solidarity and promoting group needs may be more important than rewarding individual achievements.

Finally, language differences are particularly important, and international managers must remember that not all words translate clearly into other languages. Many global companies have had difficulty crossing the language barrier, with results ranging from mild embarrassment to outright failure. For example, in regards to marketing, seemingly innocuous brand names and advertising phrases can take on unintended or hidden meanings when translated into other languages. Advertising themes often lose or gain something in translations. The English Coors beer slogan "get loose with Coors" came out as "get the runs with Coors" in Spanish. Coca-Cola's English "Coke adds life" theme translated into "Coke brings your ancestors back from the dead" in Japanese. In Chinese, the English Kentucky Fried Chicken slogan "finger-lickin' good" came out as "eat your fingers off."

Such classic boo-boos are soon discovered and corrected; they may result in little more than embarrassments for companies. Managers should keep in mind that countless other, more subtle blunders may go undetected and damage product performance in less obvious ways.

The technological environment

The technological environment contains the innovations, from robotics to cellular phones, that are rapidly occurring in all types of technology. Before a company can expect to sell its product in another country, the technology of the two countries must be compatible.

Companies that join forces with others will be able to quicken the pace of research and development while cutting the costs connected with utilizing the latest technology. Regardless of the kind of business a company is in, it must choose partners and locations that possess an available work force to deal with the applicable technology. Many companies have chosen Mexico and Mexican partners because they provide a willing and capable work force. GM's plant in Arizpe, Mexico, rivals its North American plants in quality.

Consumer safety in a global marketplace

The United States leads the world in spending on research and development. As products and technology become more complex, the public needs to know that they are safe. Thus, government agencies investigate and ban potentially unsafe products. In the United States, the Federal Food and Drug Administration has set up complex regulations for testing new drugs. The Consumer Product Safety Commission sets safety standards for consumer products and penalizes companies that fail to meet them. Such regulations have resulted in much higher research costs and in longer times between new product ideas and their introduction. This is not always true in other countries.

Functions of the International Manager

Global competition has forced businesses to change how they manage at home and abroad. The increasing rate of change, technological advances, shorter product life cycles, and high-speed communications are all factors that contribute to these changes. The new management approach focuses on establishing a new communication system that features a high level of employee involvement. Organizational structures must also be flexible enough to change with changing market conditions. Ongoing staff development programs and design-control procedures, which are understandable and acceptable, are outcomes from this new approach. Management values are changing, and managers must now have a vision and be able to communicate the vision to everyone in the firm.

Although the international manager performs the same basic functions as the domestic manager, he must adjust to more variables and environments. Therefore, each of the five basic management functions must change when operating in a foreign market.

Planning

The first stage of international planning is to decide how to do business globally: whether to export, to enter into licensing agreements or joint ventures, or to operate as a multinational corporation with facilities in a foreign country.

To develop forecasts, goals, and plans for international activities, the manager must monitor environments very closely. Key factors include political instability, currency instability, competition from governments, pressures from governments, patent and trademark protection, and intense competition.

International firms should be sure that their plans fit the culture of the host country. Typically, U.S. firms feel that long-term plans should be three to five years in length; but in some cultures, this time period is too short. Many countries must plan with the assistance of governmental agencies. As discussed in Chapter 7, working through bureaucratic structures, policies, and procedures is often time-consuming.

Organizing

International businesses must be organized so that they can adapt to cultural and environmental differences. No longer can organizations just put "carbon copies" or clones of themselves in foreign countries. An international firm must be organized so that it can be responsive to foreign customers, employees, and suppliers. An entire firm may even be organized as one giant worldwide company that has several divisions. Above all, the new organization must establish a very open communication system where problems, ideas, and grievances can quickly be heard and addressed at all levels of management. Without this, employees will not get involved, and their insights and ideas are crucial to the success of the business.

As an organization extends its operations internationally, it needs to adapt its structure. When the organization increases its international focus, it goes through the following three phases of structural change:

1. **Pre-international stage.** Companies with a product or service that incorporates the latest technology, is unique, or is superior may consider themselves ready for the international arena. The first strategy used to introduce a product to a foreign market is to find a way to export the product. At this phase, the firm adds an export manager as part of the marketing department and finds foreign partners.

2. **International division stage.** Pressure may mount through the enforcement of host country laws, trade restrictions, and competition, placing a company at a cost disadvantage. When a company decides to defend and expand its foreign market position by establishing marketing or production operations in one or more host countries, it establishes a separate international division. In turn, foreign operations begin, and a vice president, reporting directly to the president or CEO, oversees the operations.

3. **Global structure stage.** A company is ready to move away from an international division phase when it meets the following criteria:

   The international market is as important to the company as the domestic market.

   Senior officials in the company possess both foreign and domestic experience.

   International sales represent 25 to 35 percent of total sales.

   The technology used in the domestic division has far outstripped that of the international division.

As foreign operations become more important to the bottom line, decision making becomes more centralized at corporate headquarters. A functional product group, geographic approach, or a combination of these approaches should be adopted. (Chapter 7 has more information about each of these approaches.) The firm unifies international activities with worldwide decisions at world headquarters.

Staffing

Because obtaining a good staff is so critical to the success of any business, the hiring and development of employees must be done very carefully. Management must be familiar with the country's national labor laws. Next, it must decide how many managers and personnel to hire from the local labor force and whether to transfer home-based personnel.

For example, U.S. firms are better off hiring local talent and using only a few key expatriates in most cases, because the costs of assigning U.S.–based employees to positions overseas can be quite expensive. Simply, *expatriates* (people who live and work in another country) are expensive propositions even when things go well. Adding up all the extras—higher pay, airfare for family members, moving expenses, housing allowances, education benefits for the kids, company car, taxes, and home leave—means that the first year abroad often costs the multinational company many times the expatriate's base salary. The total bill for an average overseas stay of four years can easily top $1 million per expatriate. In any case, managers need to closely examine how to select and prepare expatriates.

Directing

Cultural differences make the directing function more difficult for the international manager. Employee attitudes toward work and problem solving differ by country. Language barriers also create communication difficulties. To minimize problems arising from cultural differences, organizations are training managers in cross-cultural management. Cross-cultural management trains managers to interact with several cultures and to value diversity.

In addition, the style of leadership that is acceptable to employees varies from nation to nation. In countries like France and Germany, informal relations with employees are discouraged. In Sweden and Japan, however, informal relations with employees are strongly encouraged, and a very participative leadership style is used. Incentive systems also vary tremendously. The type of incentives used in the U.S. may not work in Europe or Japan, where stable employment and benefits are more important than bonuses.

Controlling

Geographic dispersion and distance, language barriers, and legal restrictions complicate the controlling function. Meetings, reporting, and inspections are typically part of the international control system.

Controlling poses special challenges if a company engages in multinational business because of the far-flung scope of operations and the differing influences of diverse environments. Controlling operations is nonetheless a crucial function for multinational managers. In many countries, bonuses, pensions, holidays, and vacation days are legally mandated and considered by many employees as rights. Particularly powerful unions exist in many parts of the world, and their demands restrict managers' freedom to operate.

Personal Challenges for Global Managers

Building an internationally competent workforce whose members know the business and are flexible and open-minded can take years. Multinational organizations can no longer rely on just a few managers with multicultural experience or a few experts on a particular country to succeed. In short, all employees must have some minimal level of international expertise and be able to recognize cultural differences that may affect daily business communications and working relationships.

In general, overseas managers share common traits with their domestic counterparts. Wherever a manager is hired, he or she needs the technical knowledge and skills to do the job, and the intelligence and people skills to be a successful manager. Selecting managers for expatriate assignments means screening them for traits that predict success in adapting to what may be dramatically new environments.

Beyond the obvious job-specific qualifications, an organization needs to consider the following qualities and circumstances when selecting expatriates for positions in foreign countries:

- A willingness to communicate, form relationships with others, and try new things
- Good cross-cultural communication and language skills
- Flexibility and open-mindedness about other cultures
- The ability to cope with the stress of new situations
- The spouse's career situation and personal attributes

■ The existence of quality educational facilities for the candidate's children

■ Enthusiasm for the foreign assignment and a good track record in previous foreign and domestic moves

Of course, the factors that predict a successful expatriate assignment are not identical for everyone. These differences—which reflect variations in the expatriate's home culture, his or her company's human resource management practices, and the labor laws specific to the foreign country—must also be factored into the selection process.

Even if these complexities are taken into account in the selection process, a person chosen for a foreign assignment may decide not to accept the job offer. The financial package needs to be reasonably attractive. In addition, family issues may be a concern. Most candidates, after a position is offered, also want information about how the foreign posting will impact their careers.

If a potential candidate accepts the job offer, he or she should be aware of the potential for *cultural shock*—the confusion and discomfort a person experiences when in an unfamiliar culture. In addition, *ethnocentrism,* or the tendency to view one's culture as superior to others, should be understood and avoided.

Chapter Checkout

Q&A

1. Which of the following is not a proactive reason why a business becomes international?
   a. Economies of scale
   b. Searching for new customers
   c. Remaining competitive
   d. Needing raw materials and other resources

2. Which of the following is not a common characteristic of most multi-national corporations?
   a. Creating foreign affiliates that may be owned or jointly held
   b. Relying upon standardization of the product and marketing that product throughout the world
   c. Viewing the world as the market
   d. Locating affiliates in the developed countries of the world

3. Some of the major concerns of a multinational company are the stability of a country's currency and the availability of needed raw materials and supplies. These are elements of which environment?

   a. Political

   b. Legal

   c. Economic

   d. Sociocultural

4. Which of the following describes planning and the international manager?

   a. It is far less complicated for the international manager than for the manager's domestic counterpart.

   b. Planning is far more complicated for the international manager than for the manager's domestic counterpart.

   c. There is no difference in the level of difficulty between the planning in domestic and international operations.

   d. Planning is done by host-country personnel only.

5. Which of the following describes the sociocultural dilemma facing the international manager?

   a. The international manager needs only to know the culture of the host country.

   b. Most host countries require international managers to apply for citizenship in order to acquire knowledge of the culture.

   c. The manager should carefully avoid integrating the home- and host-country cultures.

   d. The international manager not only must understand the culture of the host country, but also how that culture differs from his or her home-country culture.

Answers: 1. c **2.** b **3.** c **4.** b **5.** d

CQR REVIEW

Use this CQR Review to reinforce what you've learned in this book. After you work through the review questions, you're well on your way to achieving your goal of understanding the principles of management.

Chapter 1

1. True or False: Manager skills are the abilities or capacities to use resources and/or interact with employees.

2. Which of the management functions sets the tone, impacts upon, and provides the groundwork for the other functions?
   a. Staffing
   b. Controlling
   c. Leading
   d. Coordinating
   e. Planning

3. The various levels of management in an organization are known as a(n) _____ or pyramid structure.
   a. assembly
   b. organizational process
   c. company
   d. objective
   e. hierarchy

4. Explain the relationship between managerial levels, the functions of management, managerial roles, and managerial skills.

Chapter 2

5. True or False: The primary aim of the classical scientific school was to find the "one best way" to operate.

6. True or False: Successful modern-day management practices focus upon one particular school of management theory.

7. Assuming that you are a manager, how will a knowledge of the schools of management thought help you?

Chapter 3

8. If a person is employed, his or her pay would be which type of indirect interactive force?

   a. Environmental
   b. Natural
   c. Sociocultural
   d. Technological
   e. Economic

9. Describe the internal environmental factors affecting mission, philosophy of management, leadership style, policies, formal structure, culture, climate, and resources.

Chapter 4

10. What is the most important step in the decision-making process?

11. How can managers improve their decision-making skills?

12. Which of the following is not an important contributing factor of successful brainstorming?

   a. No interruptions
   b. Feeling of freedom of expression
   c. No idea is too outlandish
   d. Free flow of ideas
   e. Groupthink

13. Bank and credit union managers would be wise to use which decision tool to accommodate walk-in "depositors" on payday?

   a. Simulation
   b. Queuing models
   c. Game theory
   d. Delphi technique
   e. Payback analysis

Chapter 5

14. True or False: The mission statement should provide the answer to why an organization exists.

15. True or False: Tactical plans are narrower in scope than strategic plans but broader in scope than operational plans.

16. True or False: The basic planning process ends with implementing the plan.

Chapter 6

17. True or False: Rules, policies, and procedures abound within the informal organization.

18. True or False: Efficient managers need not be concerned with the informal organization.

Chapter 7

19. Which of the following is not a contingency factor that affects organizational design?

   a. Strategy
   b. Size
   c. Age
   d. Function
   e. Technology

20. Real-World Scenario. The following questions and suggestions are in regards to your university/college or workplace environment:

   a. Is it mechanistic or organic in design? Explain how you reached your conclusion.
   b. What contingency factors do you think contributed to it being structured the way it is? Be specific.
   c. Explain why the organic structure is more flexible than the mechanistic structure.
   d. Describe any part of the organization that has a team structure.
   e. Describe any part of the organization that has a functional structure.
   f. Describe any part of the organization that has a matrix structure.

Chapter 8

21. Real-World Scenario. Imagine you are a newly appointed manager in any work setting. You are liable to identify things that could be done better and have many ideas that you would like to implement. Based on the ideas presented in this chapter, how should you go about effecting successful planned change in such a situation?

Chapter 9

22. True or False: The benchmark for most employment legislation within the United States is the Equal Pay Act of 1963.

23. True or False: Employee training and development are synonymous.

24. True or False: Objective performance appraisals are quantifiable and observable.

Chapter 10

25. What elements are needed for a group to be considered a team? What are the characteristics of effective teams?

26. What are vertical teams? What three types of teams are considered horizontal teams?

27. What are the four stages of team development? What occurs at each stage?

Chapter 11

28. True or False: According to Maslow, only an unsatisfied need can influence behavior.

29. True or False: Successful managers motivate individual workers in common, consistent, and collective ways.

30. True or False: The concept of job enrichment states that assigning more tasks to an employee will reduce boredom and serve as a motivational tool.

Chapter 12

31. How is management distinguished from leadership?

32. According to the contingency model of leadership effectiveness, a manager's success in leading a work group is contingent upon what factors?

33. According to the path-goal theory of leadership, what determines whether a manager's leadership style will be motivating to employees?

Chapter 13

34. Real-World Scenario. Identify a recent situation, whether in your work environment or elsewhere, in which you experienced a breakdown in communication. Utilizing the concepts presented in the text, explain the cause of the breakdown and possible methods that could have been used to prevent the breakdown.

Chapter 14

35. True or False: Controls do not have to be accepted by the members of an organization to be effective and efficient.

36. True or False: Control techniques are used to measure and monitor the performances of an organization, its people, and its processes.

Chapter 15

37. What influences over the quality of a product or service do customers really have?

38. Why must efforts to improve quality lead to increases in both productivity and profits?

Chapter 16

39. What communication problems does a firm commonly encounter when doing business in a foreign market?

40. Real-World Scenario. If you are a student, the following suggestions and questions are in regard to your college or university setting:

   a. Do some research to determine the percentage of international students.

   b. Talk with some of the international students. How is their country different politically, legally, economically, socioculturally, and technologically?

   c. Do some research to find out how your institution recruits international students.

   d. What cross-cultural considerations must the institution consider for international students? (Try to be specific.)

e. What legal requirements must the international students meet in order to attend school here?

f. Why does your institution seek international students? Interview someone in the recruitment office to find out.

g. During your interview with a recruitment person, ask how international students have changed over the last ten years.

Answers: Chapter 1: 1. T, **2.** e, **3.** e, **4.** Provide your own answer **Chapter 2: 5.** T, **6.** F, **7.** Provide your own answer **Chapter 3: 8.** e, **9.** Provide your own answer **Chapter 4: 10.** While every step is essential, proper identification of the problem is extremely critical and generally considered to be the most important step. Failure to identify the problem means that subsequent steps will not be focused on actions that result in needed solutions. **11.** Provide your own answer **12.** e, **13.** b, **Chapter 5: 14.** T, **15.** T, **16.** F, **Chapter 6: 17.** F, **18.** F, **Chapter 7: 19.** d, **20.** Provide your own answer **Chapter 8: 21.** Provide your own answer **Chapter 9: 22.** F, **23.** F, **24.** T, **Chapter 10: 25.** A team is a group of two or more people who interact regularly in a collaborative way to accomplish preset objectives and goals. **26.** A vertical team is comprised of members with various levels of authority from different tiers of management. Task force teams, cross-functional teams, and committees are all horizontal in nature. **27.** Stage 1: Individual members become acquainted during the forming stage. Stage 2: Disagreement and contrasting aspects mark the storming stage. Stage 3: The team solidifies by achieving unity during the norming stage. Stage 4: The performing stage is highlighted as the team begins to function as intended. **Chapter 11: 28.** T, **29.** F. **30.** F, **Chapter 12: 31.** Management involves performing the five management functions (planning, organizing, staffing, directing, and controlling) and using human, equipment, and information resources to achieve various objectives. Conversely, leadership focuses on getting things done through others. That is, a manager manages things (budgets, procedures, and so on), but leads others to accomplish goals. In addition, managers have legitimate power that is vested in their job descriptions, while leaders have personal power. **32.** Fred Fiedler's Contingency Model of Leadership Effectiveness states that a manager's success in leading a work group is contingent upon the task or relationship motivation (personality of the leader and the extent to which the leader has situational control and influence). In other words, success is dependent upon the personality of the leader, the abilities and personality of the team led, and the specific situation. **33.** Path-goal theory proposes that a manager's leadership style motivates to the extent that employees believe it helps them achieve things they value. This theory emphasizes the need for managers to clarify for employees the paths for obtaining goals and rewards valued by employees. **Chapter 13: 34.** Provide your own answer **Chapter 14: 35.** F, **36.** T, **Chapter 15: 37.** Provide your own answer **38.** Quality affects productivity; both quality and productivity affect profitability. The drive for one of the three must not interfere with the drive for the others. Efforts at improvement need to be coordinated and integrated. The real cost of quality is the cost of avoiding nonconformance and failure. Another cost is the cost of losing customers and wasting resources. **Chapter 16: 39.** Provide your own answer **40.** Provide your own answer

CQR RESOURCE CENTER

CQR Resource Center offers the best resources available in print and online to help you study and review the core concepts of the principles of management. You can find additional resources, plus study tips and tools to help test your knowledge, at www.cliffsnotes.com.

Books

This CliffsQuickReview book is one of many great books about management. If you want some additional resources, check out these other publications:

Reengineering Management, by James Champy, provides the guidelines managers need to lead, organize, inspire, deploy, measure, and reward as an organization continues to change. New York: Harper Business, 1995.

One-Minute Manager, by Kenneth Blanchard, Ph.D. and Spencer Johnson, M.D., is adapted from Blanchard's classic management books. A parable about a young man in search of world-class management skills, it covers goal setting, motivating, training, praising, and reprimanding employees. New York: Berkley Publishing, 1983.

In Search of Excellence, by Tom Peters and Robert Waterman, was published in 1984, but its topic is still appropriate; it provides lessons from America's best-run companies. New York: Warner Books, Inc., 1984.

On Becoming a Leader, by Warren Bennis, is a practical primer for leaders. This title provides lessons in leadership that are important for inspiring leaders in the 21st century. New York: Addison-Wesley Publishing Company, 1994.

The Fourth Wave: Business in the 21st Century, by Herman Bryant Maynard Jr. and Susan E. Mehrtens, examines important current and future changes in business. The authors emphasize the need for a new kind of leadership in a constantly changing world. San Francisco: Barrett-Koehler Publishers, 1999.

The Healing Manager, by William Lundin and Kathleen Lundin, discusses the importance of building quality relationships and productive cultures at work. This book demonstrates how a caring, concerned manager can develop a climate of trust, which results in more productivity and better quality. San Francisco: Barrett-Koehler Publishers, 1993.

Quality is Free: The Art of Making Quality Certain, by Philip B. Crosby, describes the first and only nontechnical method for installing, maintaining, and measuring a comprehensive quality improvement program in a business operation. This book emphasizes that doing things right the first time adds no additional cost to a product or service. New York: Penguin Books, 1980.

Wiley also has three Web sites that you can visit to read about all the books we publish:

- `www.cliffsnotes.com`
- `www.dummies.com`
- `www.wiley.com`

Internet

Visit the following Web sites for more information about management:

Chun Wei's Web site—`http://choo.fis.utoronto.ca`—provides an overview of historical development of management thought including planning, organizational design, motivation and leadership.

ManagerWise: Advancing the Practice of Management—`www.managerwise.com`—provides business management information and resources. It includes management resources, book reviews, news, and education opportunities.

Thingamajob.com—`www.thingamajob.com`—provides information regarding career assessment, resume writing, job hunting, and career management and development, as well as business and management developments.

Fortune.com—`www.fortune.com`—which is based on *Fortune* magazine, offers articles relating to current management issues.

Business Week Online—`www.businessweek.com`—contains current articles from *Business Week* magazine that relate to management issues.

Fast Company.com—`www.fastcompany.com`—presents the complete text from the bimonthly print magazine, *Fast Company.* The magazine covers the current revolution in how companies do business.

Next time you're on the Internet, don't forget to drop by `www.cliffsnotes.com`. We created an online Resource Center that you can use today, tomorrow, and beyond.

Glossary

acceptance theory of management principle that emphasizes the willingness of subordinates to accept those with authority to act.

accountability the answering for one's actions and accepting the consequences.

affirmative action a plan that requires employers to make an extra effort to hire and promote people who belong to a protected group.

authority the formal and legitimate right of a manager to make decisions, issue orders, and allocate resources to achieve organizational goals.

behavioral management theory a method that focuses on people as individuals with needs (also known as the human relations movement).

body language see **nonverbal communication.**

boundary spanning the process of gathering information from the external environment to identify current or likely events and determine how those events will affect the organization.

brainstorming an idea-generating process that encourages the development of alternatives while withholding criticism of those alternatives.

bureaucracy a form of organization based on logic, order, and legitimate use of formal authority.

centralized organization authority is concentrated at the top of the organization.

chain of command a line of authority that links all persons in an organization and defines who reports to whom.

charismatic power see **referent power.**

classical adminsitrative the branch of classical management theory that emphasizes the flow of information in organizations.

classical management theory a theory, developed during the Industrial Revolution, that proposes "one best way" to perform tasks. Classical management theory developed into two separate branches: the classical scientific school and the classical administrative school.

classical scientific a branch of the school of classical management theory, whose emphasis is on increasing productivity and efficiency.

closed system an organization that interacts little with its external or outside environment.

coercive power authority to punish or recommend punishment.

communication the exchange of ideas, messages, or information, by speech, signals, or writing.

compensation all work-related payments, including wages, commissions, insurance, and other benefits.

competitive advantage any aspect of an organization that distinguishes it from its competitors in a positive way.

condition of certainty situation that occurs when the decision maker has perfect knowledge of all the information needed to make a decision.

content theory identifies physical or psychological conditions that act as stimuli for human behavior.

contingency planning development of alternative courses of action that can be implemented if and when the original plan proves inadequate because of changing circumstances.

contingency theory this principle examines the fit between the leader and the situation and provides guidelines for managers to achieve an effective fit (also known as situational theory).

continuous process a system that produces goods by continuously feeding raw materials through highly automated technology.

control the systematic process of regulating organization activities to make them consistent with the expectations established in plans, targets, and standards of performance.

concurrent control method of regulation applied to processes as they are happening.

cost-leadership strategy system that focuses on keeping costs as low as possible through efficient operations and tight controls.

crisis problem an unexpected problem that has the potential to lead to disaster if not resolved quickly and appropriately.

cross-functional teams groups of experts in various specialties (or functions) who work together on solutions to organizational problems.

decentralized organizations firms that consciously attempt to spread authority to the lowest possible levels.

decision tree a diagram that analyzes hiring, marketing, investment, equipment purchases, pricing, and similar decisions. Decision trees assign probabilities to each possible outcome and calculate payoffs for each decision path.

delegation the downward transfer of authority from a manager to a subordinate.

demographics measurements of various characteristics of the people and social groups who make up a society.

development plans a series of steps that can help employees acquire skills to reach long-term goals, such as job promotions.

differentiation strategy a plan whereby a company attempts to set the organization's products or services apart form those of other companies.

division of labor see **work specialization.**

embargo a prohibition on trade in a particular area.

employee benefits legally required or voluntary compensation provided to employees in addition to their salaries.

empowerment giving individuals in an organization autonomy.

expectancy theory a motivational theory stating that the three factors that influence behavior are the value of the reward, the relationship of the reward to performance, and the effort required for performance

expert power a leader's special knowledge or skills regarding the tasks performed by followers.

exporting selling of an organization's products to a foreign broker or agent.

feedforward controls method used to identify and prevent defects and deviations from standards.

financial audits formal investigations to ensure that procedures, policies, laws, and ethical guidelines are followed in the handling and reporting of financial activities.

financial ratio analysis the relationship between specific figures on an organization's financial statements; helps explain the significance of those figures.

financial statements reports that provide management with information to monitor financial resources.

first-line management the lowest level of management.

flexiplace see **telecommuting.**

flextime work an employment alternative that allows employees to decide, within a certain range, when to begin and end each work day.

force-field analysis a technique to implement change by determining which forces drive change and which forces resist it.

formal structure the hierarchical arrangement of tasks and people within an organization.

functional authority authority to make decisions about specific activities undertaken by personnel in other departments.

functional structure an organizational design that groups positions into departments on the basis of the specialized activities of the business.

functional teams work groups that perform specific organizational functions with members from several vertical levels of the hierarchy.

grapevine the informal communications network within an organization (also known as **social network** and **informal channels**).

horizontal job loading see **job enlargement.**

human relations movement see **behavioral management theory.**

incentive pay links compensation and performance by paying employees for actual results, not for seniority or hours worked.

income statement a report that presents the difference between an organization's income and expenses to determine whether the firm operated at a profit or loss over a specified time.

informal channels see **grapevine.**

informal organization the pattern, behavior, and interaction that stems from personal rather than official relationships.

interpersonal communication real-time, face-to-face, or voice-to-voice conversation that allows immediate feedback.

intrapreneurship organizational culture that allows employees flexibility and authority in pursuing and developing new ideas.

job analysis a study that determines all tasks and qualifications needed for each position.

job description a written statement of a job's requirements, processes, and rationale.

job enlargement a type of job redesign that increases the variety of tasks a position includes (also known as horizontal job loading).

job enrichment a type of job redesign that not only includes an increased variety of tasks, but also provides the employee with more responsibility and authority (also known as vertical job loading).

job rotation temporarily assigning employees to different job, or tasks to different people, on a rotating basis.

job sharing process in which one full-time job is split between two or more persons (also known as twinning).

joint venture a business relationship formed between a domestic and foreign firm.

kaizen a Japanese term used in the business setting to mean incremental, continuous improvement.

leading establishing and influencing others to follow a specific direction.

learning organizations firms that utilize people, values, and systems to continuously change and improve performance based on the lessons of experience.

legitimate power vested authority stemming from a formal management position in an organization.

licensure agreement contract that grants one firm the right to make or sell another company's products.

line authority a manager's right to direct the work of his or her employees and make decisions without consulting others.

liquidity ratios measurements of an organization's ability to generate cash.

management the process of administering and coordinating resources effectively, efficiently, and in an effort to achieve the goals of the organization.

management information systems (MIS) collects, organizes, and distributes data in such a way that the information meets managers' needs.

manager a person responsible for the work performance of one or more other persons.

mass production a system used to manufacture a large number of uniform products in an assembly line.

means-end chain the effective design of organizational goals that encourages the accomplishment of low-level goals as a way of achieving high-level goals.

mechanistic structure a highly bureaucratic organizational method, with centralized authority, detailed rules and procedures, a clear-cut division of labor, narrow span of controls, and formal coordination.

mission statement a document that describes what an organization stands for and why it exists.

motion study research designed to isolate the best possible method of performing a given job.

multinational corporations (MNC) organizations operating facilities in one or more countries.

need theory a construct of motivation based upon physical or psychological conditions that act as stimuli for human behavior.

network structure an operating process that relies on other organizations to perform critical functions on a contractual basis.

nonverbal communication actions, gestures, and other aspects of physical appearance that can be a powerful means of transmitting messages (also known as body language).

ongoing plans see **continuing plans.**

open system a method in which an individual or organization must interact with various and constantly changing components in both the external and internal environments.

operational goals specific, measurable results expected from first-level managers, work groups, and individuals.

operational plan developed by a first level supervisor as the means to achieve operational objectives in support of tactical plans.

organic structure a management system founded on cooperation and knowledge-based authority.

organization a group of individuals who work together to accomplish a common goal.

organizational change a significant change that affects an entire company.

organizational chart a pictorial display of the official lines of authority and communication within an organization.

organizational climate the byproduct of organizational culture; it is the barometer for determining the morale of the employees.

organizational culture an organization's personality.

organizational design the creation or change of an organization's structure, the configuration and interrelationships of positions and departments.

organizational development (OD) a plan that focuses on changing an entire organization by changing processes and organizational culture.

organizing the process of establishing the orderly use of resources by assigning and coordinating tasks.

orientation a socialization process designed to provide necessary information to new employees and welcome them into the organization.

performance appraisal a formal, structured system designed to measure an employee's job performance against designated standards.

philosophy of management a manager's set of personal beliefs and values about people and work.

plan a blueprint for goal achievement that specifies the necessary resource allocations, schedules, tasks, and other actions.

planned change the deliberate structuring of operations and behaviors in anticipation of environmental forces.

planning the act of determining the organization's goals and defining the means for achieving them.

privacy laws legal rights of employees regarding who has access to information about their work history and job performance.

procedure a set of step-by-step directions that explain how activities or tasks are to be carried out.

process theories rationales that attempt to explain how workers select behavioral actions to meet their needs and determine their choices.

profitability ratios measurements of an organization's ability to generate profits.

quality reflects the degree to which a goods or services meets the demands and requirements of the marketplace.

quantitative approach using quantitative techniques, such as statistics, information models, and computer simulations, to improve decision making.

queuing theory a rationale that helps allocate services or workstations to minimize customer waiting and service cost.

quotas government regulations that limit the import of specific products within the year.

recruitment activities an organization uses to attract a pool of viable candidates.

reengineering redesigning processes requiring input from every employee in the company to achieve dramatic improvements in cost, quality, service, and speed.

referent power influence that results from leadership characteristics that command identification, respect, and admiration from subordinates (also known as charismatic power).

resources the people, information, facilities, infrastructure, machinery, equipment, supplies, and finances at an organization's disposal.

reward power the authority to reward others.

risk the environment that exists when a manager must make a decision without complete information.

rule an explicit statement that tells a supervisor what he or she can and cannot do.

satisfice the making of the best decision possible with the information, resources, and time available.

scalar principle a system that demonstrates a clearly defined line of authority in the organization that includes all employees.

selective perception the tendency to single out for attention those aspects of a situation or person that reinforce or appear consistent with one's existing beliefs, values, or needs.

self-fulfilling prophecy a belief that a manager can, through his or her behavior, create a situation where subordinates act in ways that confirm his or her original expectations.

simulation a broad term indicating any type of activity that attempts to imitate an existing system or situation in a simplified manner.

situational theory see **contingency theory.**

small-batch production manufacturing of a variety of custom, made-to-order products.

social network see **grapevine.**

strategic change revision that takes place when a company changes its tactics (strategy)—possibly even its mission statement—to achieve current goals.

strategic plan an outline of steps designed with the goals of the entire organization as a whole in mind, rather than with the goals of specific divisions or departments.

structural change variation that occurs when a company changes its procedures, policies, and rules, and as a result, its organizational structure.

structured problems familiar, straightforward, and clear difficulties with respect to the information needed to resolve them.

tactical plan steps detailing the actions needed to achieve the organization's larger strategic plan.

tariffs taxes placed on imports and/or exports in response to a political event.

team structure organizational design that places separate functions into a group according to one overall objective.

technology the knowledge, machinery, work procedures, and materials that transform inputs into outputs.

telecommuting a work arrangement that allows at least a portion of scheduled work hours to be completed outside of the office, with work at home as one of the options (also known as flexiplace).

Total Quality Management (TQM) a philosophy that states that uniform commitment to quality in all areas of the organization promotes a culture that meets consumers' perceptions of quality.

twinning see **job sharing.**

unity of command principle that states that an employee should have one and only one supervisor to whom he or she is directly responsible.

unstructured problems difficulties that involve ambiguities and information deficiencies and often occur as new or unexpected situations.

validity proof that the relationship between a selection device and some relevant job criterion exists.

vertical job loading see **job enrichment.**

vision   the ability of the leader to bind people together with an idea.

wholly-owned subsidiary   a foreign firm owned outright, or with a controlling interest, by an out-of-country firm.

work specialization   the degree to which organizational tasks are divided into separate jobs (also known as the division of labor).

zero defects   a program that emphasizes doing it right the first time.

Index